BOOK PUBLICITY FOR AUTHORS AND PUBLISHERS

- Radio
- Television

Larry J. Rochester
Media Producer, Talk Show Host, Publicist

A Sunset Hill Book

BOOK PUBLICITY FOR AUTHORS AND PUBLISHERS
- Radio
- Television

by

Larry J. Rochester

Published by:
> Sunset Hill
> Fall River Mills, CA

All rights Reserved. No part of this book is to be reproduced or transmitted in any form or by any means, electronic or mechanical, including photocopying, recording or by any information storage and retrieval system without written permission from Sunset Hill, except for the inclusion of brief quotations in a review. This book was printed using soy ink.

Copyright © 1992 by Sunset Hill.
> First Printing 1992
> Printed in the United States of America

Library of Congress Cataloging-in- Publication Data

Rochester, Larry J., 1944-
> Book Publicity for Authors and Publishers: radio, television / Larry J. Rochester.
> p. cm.
> Includes bibliographical references and index.
> 1-88-1447-00-6

> 1. Authorship–Marketing. 2. Mass media. 3. Self-publishing. 4. Little presses. I. Title.

Z278.R6 1992   302.23
                              QBI92-10776

Library of Congress Catalog Card #92-90859

ISBN: 1-881447-00-6

About The Author

Larry Rochester is an award-winning photographer who has worked in the media as a disc-jockey, talk show host, producer, radio station manager, publicist, journalist and magazine features editor. A people-oriented person, Larry has also worked in sales and owned a small public relations firm.

In 1969, Larry had his first exposure to broadcasting over a small cable FM station in a beach community on the California coast. Since that time, he has produced and hosted shows over numerous radio and television stations throughout the state.

Larry retired in early 1991 and began to write full-time. He is working on a fiction novel about a talk show host who sets out to change the world ... and does, plus a companion work to this book, intended primarily for small organizations.

For those who envision a new tomorrow,
that the world might be a better place for us all.

DISCLAIMER

This is a guidebook through the media maze that can lead to getting almost free publicity through radio, TV and the press. The book is intended for self-published authors and owners of small presses. This book is a guidebook only and is not to be construed as being the ultimate source to media publicity or as legal advice from the publisher or author.

The techniques described within this book have worked for the author and for others that he knows. However, their effectiveness depends upon the talent and determination of the individual applying the techniques plus the receptiveness of individual media sources. Because the the human element must enter into the equation, the publisher and author cannot make any guarantees as to actual media response.

The author believes the material contained herein is accurate. However, Sunset Hill and the author shall have neither liability nor responsibility to any person or entity with respect to any loss or damage caused, or alleged to be caused, directly or indirectly, by the information contained herein.

DISCLAIMER

Table of Contents

Introduction 1
1 - The Publicist 3
2 - The Media Database 9
3 - The Teaser Message 19
4 - The Producer's Point of View 29
5 - Stations and Their Interview Shows 37
6 - Fliers and News Releases 43
7 - Scheduling Interviews 49
8 - The Follow-Up Call 65
9 - The Art Of Being Interviewed 71
10 - Show Time! 93
11 - After The Interview 113
12 - The Publicity Tour 117
13 - Step-By-Step Procedures: A Review 127
Appendix 133
    Glossary 135
    Bibliography 151
    Acknowledgements 153
    About The Author 155
    Index 157

Introduction

This is the 'how to' of low-budget media publicity, a book that mainly deals with radio and television talk shows; how to line them up and do them like a professional. It is also a book about getting reviews in print. This book has been written primarily for self-published authors and owners of small presses who may not have the necessary means to hire a professional publicist or to appear in an interview availability listing magazine. Using the system outlined in this book, the media can become accessible for relatively little money.

Many of the techniques contained herein are those professional publicists know and use to get media coverage for their clients. The system in this book has been perfected through practical experience and is capable of a high degree of workability if applied correctly. To make the media work, one does not have to be a professional publicist … just act that way.

One prime concept that must be fully grasped, if one is to be successful at the media publicity game, is that our only limitations are those that we have agreed to. If we say, "It can't be done," then *sure enough* it can't. Richard Bach talks about this in <u>Illusions:</u> Argue for your limitations and they will become yours… but reverse that and anything becomes possible.

The book should be carefully read, and the techniques grasped completely, before any attempt is made at working with the media. To do otherwise could lead to some basic concepts being misunderstood, and this could open the door to their misapplication and a loss of possible media coverage which, of course, is counter-productive.

The essential information in this book is justified to the left-hand margin.

Personal anecdotes and optional information are offset to the right. This format is used to cover much of my experience on both sides of the microphone.

A comprehensive media glossary and index is included in the Appendix.

    Larry J. Rochester

Chapter 1

The Publicist

Writing books is most often a solo affair, but when dealing with publicity, it's best to have some assistance: a publicist.

Now, the author can always go out and pay a professional publicist $1,000 or more a month, or a close friend or partner can be recruited for the job. In either event, it's going to take two people to get the job done correctly. With that in mind, the focus of this chapter is the amateur publicist.

For some reason, many producers are turned off by authors calling directly for interview bookings.

When authors call for their own bookings, many producers feel this looks amateurish; in their way of thinking a successful author should be able to afford a publicist. Following their reasoning, if the author is not successful, why should they put him or her on the air?

Also, most of the publishing houses have professional publicists. So, the need is for the self-published author to have one as well.

The publicist can make or break a publicity effort and must be picked with care.

The only real requirements are that the publicist be dedicated to the author and the project, have a professional attitude, a good working knowledge of the media (this book will provide that), and be adaptable.

The publicist should also be able to communicate with just about anyone and have *no reservations whatsoever* about contacting the media.

The publicist should be a perfectionist at his or her work. Especially important is the ability to shrug off failure, dig in and keep going no matter what. This ability must be tempered with the wisdom to know when it is wise to withdraw and reconsider the course of action.

A good publicist will fall into the craft quite naturally, whereas the wrong person will continually struggle and clearly be out of his or her element. With that in mind, I think it can be safely said that people either have what it takes or they don't.

Throughout the years, I have seen more destructive PRs and publicists than I care to think about. More often than not, the havoc they have created is not brought about by malice, but simply by being the wrong person for the job.

Let's take a look at what a publicist or PR person is and is not. The common perception of a publicist or PR person is often something of a cross between a fast talking salesman and a con man. This is complicated by newspaper help-wanted ads for 'PR Trainees' whose main job will be one of door-to-door or telephone sales. Such stereotypes have little reality in the actual world of media publicity. Granted, some PRs and publicists would fit into the above picture very well but, fortunately, they are in the minority.

Success comes to those who not only believe in it but are willing to work for it.

Public relations and publicity work is just that: a lot of work. That's not to say that it isn't fun or doesn't have its rewards, but it can take a lot out of a person. Yet the successful PR person, the successful publicist, keeps going despite it all.

Fortunately, when we're looking to publicize a particular book, we aren't necessarily counting on repeat interviews over a period of time as we would be for other topics, such as environmental issues.

I'm a great believer in the power of the mind and I've trusted in that power to get me through many a rough time. But, it's a funny universe we live in ... occasionally, we have to nudge it a little. Sometimes things have to be <u>made</u> to go right.

Dr. Earl Babbie made a most interesting comment when I interviewed him regarding his book, <u>You Can Make A Difference</u>. He stated that the hardest step of a journey is, quite often, not the first step but the *second*. That makes a lot of sense to me, and in light of what we are discussing here, it bears some consideration.

The good publicist knows this instinctively and will take that second step without even thinking about it, trusting in his or her own ability to forge ahead and make everything come out right. One simple point to remember: If you fall flat on your face you are, at worst, pointing in the right direction ... forward.

The job requires someone who is willing to pay the price. Dedication is the key, but equally important is persistence and a determination to do the job right.

Because the publicist should accompany the author for any media interview, the job sometimes requires very long hours. When the campaign gets rolling, it's fairly common to attend one or two interviews before noon, a couple more in the afternoon, and possibly a personal appearance or two in the evening.

Of course, what is described above is not the typical day, but it's important for the publicist to be aware of the fact that it could be and be willing to do whatever is necessary towards that end.

When beginning the publicity campaign, there's just no getting around the fact that it's going to take a lot of work to get things rolling. This means a lot of telephone calls, letters, press kits and hitting the air waves and the print media again and again. It takes a lot of persistence. But for those who persist, the rewards are there.

The publicist (and author) should always remember, that when dealing with the media, they are working with show business, and in the tradition of show business, the show *must go on*.

A show's host will not be thrilled by a last minute cancellation. If a cancellation becomes necessary, the publicist should try to do it *at least* three or four days in advance - the more time the better. Hopefully, the interview can be rescheduled.

For a producer and show host, there is nothing so aggravating as a last minute cancellation or, worse yet, a 'no-show.'

When dealing with people in the media, remember that their time is valuable. When offered an interview, the publicist and author should treat the opportunity as if it were made of gold because, in a manner of speaking, it is. Interviews bring responses and responses can translate directly into books being sold.

Attention must always be paid as to how the media is approached.

Like every other media producer, I have been contacted for interviews by publicists or by potential guests themselves who have either insulted me over the phone, or almost put me to sleep. Personally, it is beyond me how anyone who is seeking free publicity could ever allow representation by such an individual.

Long ago I decided to not book interviews with such people *regardless of how interesting the proposed subject might be*.

A bit unfair? Well, maybe, but experience taught me that boring or insulting publicists or authors will *almost always* give similar interviews. As a result, I learned to save myself a lot of trouble by simply refusing to work with such people.

Not wearing the publicist hat properly can, and often will, prevent favorable media exposure.

The publicist must be extremely knowledgeable on the topic of the book. It's also important for the publicist to be a quick thinker and able to project *totally* into the communication of the message. The better this is done, the better the chances of lining up interviews.

Again, the publicist must have absolutely no reservations about contacting media stations or the press. If those reservations exist, then it is best for the author to consider someone else for the job. This is vital, for the media contacts are just too important to have them blown away by incompetence.

However, it must be noted that the opposite attitude can also put a stop to free publicity.

Pushy prima donnas who try to impress everyone with their 'expertise,' can quickly turn off producers and editors.

Only one person should be contacting the media. First of all, this is not a job that lends itself to a group effort, and the personal touch is often the determining factor in getting bookings. One person, willing to work, can easily handle a major metropolitan area. Get more than one person on this job and problems begin to appear in rapid succession because there are just too many things that can go wrong.

If many different cities are involved, such as in a national publicity tour, then separate, *properly trained*, people can work with different regional or metropolitan areas. The scheduling can be done separately, but should have central coordination.

> While on a trip to Chicago, I attempted to set up a few interviews for my client. Media appearances were not the primary reason for going to Chicago and his schedule had been uncertain at the time, so we waited until we arrived to schedule the media appearances around his other activities. The only exception to this was a news conference held the first day.

Rochester

Imagine my surprise when I found out that one of our Chicago contacts had already attempted to line up air time the day before ... and this was a lady who knew very little about what she was doing. In fact, she had managed to alienate several potential media sources prior to our arrival!

Of course she hadn't told us about it. She meant well, I'm sure, but she had an abrasive, pushy personality and it simply turned off many of the producers.

Luckily, I managed to salvage most of the stations, and we ended up doing several TV and newstalk radio shows in the month that we were there.

The moral, of course, is get the right person on the job, for the wrong person will cause so many problems and create so many upsets that he or she just isn't worth the trouble. Quite often, someone who just can't cut it as a publicist can be utilized without problems in some other area, such as shipping.

Chapter 2

The Media Database

Throughout the United States there are over ten thousand radio and television stations that can be utilized for publicity purposes. Likewise, thousands of newspapers, periodicals, and cable-television stations offer access to the general public.

Pick any point in the country, draw a circle with a radius of 75 or 100 miles around it and ferret out the number of media outlets within it. In a very real sense, the possibilities are virtually unlimited, and where not unlimited, certainly impressive.

From March of 1982 through April of 1985, I worked as publicist for a private counseling center in Burlingame, California that was offering a revolutionary new therapy for learning disabilities. The 37 months spent promoting that one client mainly throughout California proved what a determined media effort could accomplish.

During that time, the organization completed over 112 hours of interview air time on radio and television. That's a little under 3.5 hour's air time a month; the average interview was about 20 minutes in length. In addition, the client received an average of over 20 column inches of favorable press each month. Such exposure, had the client paid for it, could have easily cost over a million dollars!

The above was accomplished with a minimum of telephone calls, printing, postage, and travel expenses.

While one must of course factor in the time consumed in writing news releases, mailing out press kits and such, the average interview still only cost the center somewhere in the vicinity of $20 per interview. (Compare that with commercial air time easily costing over $100-300 per 30 second spot in the San Francisco area.) The center reached millions of people with its message, for a comparatively small amount of money.

The Media Plan

Before a comprehensive media plan can be worked out and acted upon, the area of operation must be defined. Once that has been done, a course of action must be determined that will allow the media sources within that area to be fully utilized.

Unlike organizations, authors will likely get only one shot at any given media source per book because repeat interviews or coverage is unlikely. With this in mind, it is best to get the maximum coverage out of a given area.

Be realistic about the area of operation!

Authors have a decision to make when selecting the area of operation. Should media sources be approached just locally, regionally, state wide or on a national basis? There is always the temptation to shoot for the stars ... but remember: travel takes time and *time truly is money.*

Information must be gathered on each media source within the planned area of operation.

Having determined the area of operation, media resources within that area need to be researched in the following categories:
1. Radio stations
2. TV stations
3. Cable TV stations that offer public access
4. Radio, TV and cable TV network availability:
   (A show might be produced locally but have regional or national air play.)
5. Newspapers: Daily, Weekly, and Biweekly
   (Don't ignore even the small 'throw away' type of papers, for people do read them and will often respond to an article or review in such a paper.)
6. Locally-produced Magazines

7. Newsletters:
   (Many corporate, private or organizational newsletters carry book reviews.)

The Media Files

The media files are important and must not be approached in a haphazard manner if the publicity effort is to be successful.

Keeping the files straight is a job in itself, and is crucial to getting the job done correctly.

Granted as authors, we perhaps shun the business side of things; "I'm an artist! Just let me create!" Well, okay, but basic files do have to be set up and used. This is where the publicist comes into play.

Up-to-date media files are, arguably, the most effective publicity tools possible. Typically, they will contain pertinent information regarding each media source within a given area.

When promoting nationally, files need to be maintained for only specific sources in each city (unless the plan is to approach *each* media source). These would normally be the big (i.e. network) radio and TV stations and major publications.

For simplicity's sake, the files can be kept on standard 3x5 cards (for our purposes here, 'media cards') and on any standard size ruled paper. Of course this information can also be stored in a personal computer or electronic notebook.

Away from the office, new information can be written on the back of a business card, although it is best to always carry the media cards plus a few blanks. (Details of this card system come later in this chapter.)

The author and publicist should not rely on memory alone! Information should be written down *as it is received* and then added to the appropriate file as soon as possible. The files can function as a media memory.

A duplicate copy of all outgoing and the original of any

incoming correspondence regarding each media source should be placed in the appropriate media file.

All phone calls should be noted on a sequential log in the appropriate media file. It's a good idea to take notes during phone calls and then expand them immediately after the call.

Always review the appropriate file before speaking to any media contact. Update the file immediately thereafter.

When the files are complete, what has been created is a media database. The information in the database is instantly available for inspection or referral. The importance of this is obvious. It's important to know who to talk to at the stations or newspapers. It's equally important to know about interview appointments and directions.

If the files are not organized, publicity efforts can quickly go downhill due to missed appointments and interviews.

Needless to say, this is self-defeating. The importance of keeping the database up to date becomes evident when 50 or 60 media sources need to be approached and dealt with. For that matter, even five or six stations can create a major headache if the database is not current.

This sounds like (and can be) a lot of work. But if a large number of media sources are being approached, keeping the files straight is vital to getting the job done. It also makes life much easier. If notes are kept simple, a page can be quickly scanned and the overall picture of what has previously transpired becomes immediately clear. This is especially important when a media contact calls and asks for additional information, as the entire conversation must often be handled 'on the fly.' The need is one of knowing what was previously said.

> One day, early in my promotions career, a station called requesting an interview with an organization I represented. Just as this was happening another station called, also requesting an interview. I hastily agreed to the interview with the first station, dutifully noting down the time and date on

my desk calendar. I then took the call from the second station and scheduled another interview, planning to update both files afterwards.

That was my first mistake.

Immediately after the second call I got involved in yet another. I was getting in deeper and deeper yet, curiously I felt in complete control.

Needless to say, I blew it.

The last two interviews went fine, but with the first station … well, let's just say that the day arrived and we were ready to go … where? In my haste, I had forgotten to note down the first station's call letters or address! Somewhere that day, a producer was wondering where his (at least I remembered the proper gender) guests were.

Once a producer has been stood up by an organization or individual, he or she will seldom offer a second invitation. My screw-up cost my client the opportunity to reach thousands of people. And with that terrible screw-up, the client was effectively stopped to that degree. When media people begin to respond, the object of their interest has suddenly become 'hot' to them. It's a mistake to let their interest cool off. I've never forgotten that lesson, and it bears keeping in mind: air time is quite literally, 'worth its weight in gold.'

No matter how busy the day or moment, always be available for phone calls from media people.

Do not **keep media contacts waiting.**

It's important for the publicist to answer all phone messages or letters promptly. Trying to juggle incoming and outgoing information can be next to impossible if the information is not written down *as it is obtained* and then filed correctly thereafter.

If not already, the publicist should become an avid record keeper … then protect those records like a mother lion protecting her cubs!

Reference Books

Reference books are invaluable for media publicity work. My two favorites are listed below but, in fairness to other publishers, it should be noted that there are other books available which do the same basic job as the two listed below. In addition, there are also books that focus on specific geographic areas and media formats. Reference books may be ordered direct from the publisher or usually found in the reference section of any large library.

Broadcasting & Cable Marketplace is an excellent overall source book for the broadcast industry. It contains complete listings for radio, TV, and Cable TV stations.

Gale Directory of Publications and Broadcast Media (Formerly IMS/AYER Directory of Publications) is similar to the broadcasting/cablecasting yearbook mentioned above, but lists newspapers and other publications.

A word of caution: Don't take the information contained in any media reference book as absolute gospel, as things can and often do, change between issues. This is especially true in the volatile world of radio. *Always* **call for the appropriate names.**

At the risk of being redundant, let me state that I cannot stress too highly the importance of keeping the database up-to-date. The easy way is to keep the files current and properly arranged. If the job is being done correctly, the files will reflect an up-to-date picture of everything that has previously transpired with any media contact. The importance of this becomes evident when a radio or TV station is interested in booking the author for an appearance, but cannot do so for a couple of months: the publicist needs to know *when* to call back and *who* to ask for.

The Media Database

Ordinary 3x5 cards, ruled or unruled, and letter-sized file folders are the essence of the system outlined in this book. The file folders contain the sequential contact logs and copies of all incoming and outgoing correspondence and similar notations of phone calls.

The media cards are easy to use, and if necessary, several hundred can be carried at one time without taking up too much space in a briefcase. Their small size can be an important asset while on the road.

Several years ago I was in Los Angeles for a week-long publicity tour with a client that included television, radio and newspaper interviews plus personal appearances. Anyone who has ever been to Los Angeles will know just how large that area is and how long it can take to travel from one end to the other. A typical day saw us leaving Santa Monica in the morning and driving to Long Beach for one interview, then traveling northeast to Pasadena for another, then over to Hollywood and back into L.A. proper. Sounds easy, but each interview was miles apart ... and on the infamous L.A. freeways, where gridlock is a way of life!

The cards required for this trip were very specialized.

As soon as the itinerary was set, I obtained directions, *in sequence* from each stop to the next, and wrote the directions on the back of the individual cards. The cards were then numbered appropriately in pencil (i.e. Tuesday, #3). It became a simple matter of following the directions on each card. If we ran into a situation where a station had to cancel or wanted to reschedule us for later, then I simply made the changes on our itinerary and adjusted the cards accordingly.

Along with a good map, the media cards proved to be lifesavers and allowed us to maintain each day's schedule with a minimum amount of fuss. Equally important was that our directions, numbered sequentially from one stop to the next, were given to us by our contacts. They knew which freeways to avoid at what times of the day and the easiest way around town.

Let the media cards do the work!

The next step is to look up the basic information regarding the media sources in the planned area(s) of operation and then build the database with this information, either in a computer or on the media cards.

The individual listings should include the city, the media source name or call letters (i.e. Sacramento Bee, WKRP AM, NBC TV), the station frequency, the primary personnel (producers, show hosts, reporters, etc.) the address, directions, and any other pertinent information. It's not necessary to get elaborate with this, but it does help to be consistent with the style in which the cards are created. The media cards are not intended to be as thorough, or contain as much information as the rest of the files, but they are vital to any publicity job.

The various books listing radio and TV stations contain a lot of information that is not needed for publicity purposes, such as a given station's antenna height and national advertising representative. The only information necessary to publicity efforts is as listed above. As mentioned previously, it's not a good idea to simply accept the names or call letters listed in these guide books as being accurate. Publishers of media reference books go to great lengths to ensure the accuracy of their information but changes can, and do, occur. It's best to first list the information and then follow-up with a phone call to the station or publication to verify accuracy.

Most of the reference books will contain information regarding a given station or publication's advertising rates. This can be helpful in determining the popularity of a given media source. The rule of thumb is this: the higher the rate, the more popular the source. In the highly competitive media market, stations or publications with low ratings cannot, as a general rule, get away with charging high rates. That is simply because the advertising clients, wanting more 'bang for their buck' will not pay them. Note that non-commercial stations will not have advertising rates, yet are invariably popular.

It has recently become a fad within the broadcast industry for radio stations to go by slogans or 'logo I.D.s' that reflect their assigned frequency rather than their call letters, such as KFRC AM in San Francisco going by 'Magic 61' for its frequency of 610 kilohertz. These slogan identifiers are also sometimes extended to reflect the format, such as KGO AM radio, with a frequency of 810 kilohertz, going by 'Newstalk Radio 81.' It's helpful to list these identifiers on the cards as well.

The publicist should ensure that accurate and clear directions are written on the back of the media cards in pencil. Clarity, especially regarding directions, is crucial.

Many of the media source books list radio and television stations by the 'city of origin' (where the station's *broadcast studios* are located) and the 'city of license.' It's important to know the difference as the two are not necessarily the same and can (especially with radio stations) sometimes be as much as fifty miles apart.

Ignore the 'city of license' listings in media reference books. For all practical purposes, the *only* address listing that has any meaning for publicity purposes is the *'city of origin.'*

In today's market, many stations and publications are co-owned ... owned by one corporation. Separate cards are needed for the files, but only one needs to be maintained with directions and such - *providing that the stations broadcast from the same location and share common call letters,* such as KFRC AM & FM in San Francisco.

The best way to label the file folders in the database is to simply indicate the call letters (or publication name) and frequency on the tab, and then the city of origin underneath.

List the frequency both on the card and on the file folder. This is important, as *stations can change their call signs, but as a general rule, the frequency will not change.*

Formats should be individually listed unless the stations are 'simulcasting' (duplicating) the format on both stations. If that is the case, the media cards should reflect it. However, if the stations are co-owned but operate as separate entities and at different locations, then separate cards will need to be maintained.

Rochester

After the cards and file folders have been completed, with each media station, publication, newspaper, news service and accessible cable station listed, they should be filed alphabetically.

All normal broadcast stations in the United States have call letters that begin with 'W' or 'K.' (Canadian stations begin with a 'C' and Mexican stations begin with an 'X.')

The only time stations are listed differently in the U.S. is when they are 'translator stations.' Translator stations are essentially stations that are limited to low power and are used to rebroadcast the signals of normal broadcast stations, thereby extending their signals into rural areas where reception is poor.

Translator stations that serve radio stations will not normally have their own studios, whereas TV translators may.

Low Power Television Station (LPTV) status is sometimes granted by the FCC to a TV translator station, allowing it to originate programming to serve a very specific (and usually rural) area.

Any programming that may be initiated over translator stations cannot, by law, interfere with programming over regularly scheduled stations, but may focus on community-oriented formats. The broadcast reference books list such stations.

The point is that an LPTV station might have an interview show or two which can be accessed.

Chapter 3

The Teaser Message

(Note: From this point on, we will be discussing how to work with media producers and print editors. Because my orientation is primarily with radio and television, I'll speak mainly in those terms. However, it should be understood that the same techniques used to line up electronic media can also be used for print interviews.)

In Chapter Two, we discussed undertaking a thorough evaluation of the possibilities for interview coverage in a given area. Such an evaluation is important in that it provides an idea, however basic, of the potential involved. It also serves as a basis for any media work to follow.

As important as knowing which stations and publications to approach is, simply put, what is there to talk about? The book ... right? Well, yes and no. "Sort of," would be the best answer. This is where having a teaser message comes into play.

Most books couldn't be read over the air in a thirty-minute period. At best, at very best, a condensation - a teaser message - is all that can be imparted. It's just like going fishing in that, to catch anything, you've got to bait the hook or throw a lure.

In an interview of any length, the show host will take up a certain amount of time introducing the show, the book and the author. The author's credentials must also be established. There are quite naturally pauses. There might be station breaks or commercials. The show host will comment on the author's answers.

All these things chew up time. The actual amount of time the author has to talk about his or her book is precious little.

A thirty-minute 'interview,' isn't necessarily that; the term is misleading. The term actually refers to the *time slot* the show or segment occupies.

Out of a straight thirty-minute interview in which the author is the sole person being interviewed, he or she might get to talk about the book for only ten minutes or so, when all the above factors are figured in.

In a ten-minute segment of a television program, the author might be actually speaking for only three or four minutes.

It's important to remember that time spent on the air just seems to fly by, and this is another reason for having a well thought out, brief teaser message.

When on the air, the answer to any interview question must reflect the teaser message and the topic of the book. Whenever possible, the answer should also be about something the audience can relate to directly.

Care must be taken to ensure that the this teaser message is a complete concept.

It's not a good idea to leave the audience dangling off a cliff ... the idea is to bring them to a point where they become sufficiently interested to seek out the book.

Let's look at a couple of hypothetical interview questions:

Interview Question:

"Why did you write this book, Larry?

Answer:

"Well, Jane, I wrote BOOK PUBLICITY FOR AUTHORS AND PUBLISHERS as an answer to a problem faced by many self-published authors ... namely that it's *terribly* expensive to publish your own book and most self-published authors may not have the money to spend $1,000 a month or more for a professional publicist.

BOOK PUBLICITY FOR AUTHORS AND PUBLISHERS

"BOOK PUBLICITY FOR AUTHORS AND PUBLISHERS *solves* that problem and shows them how to get on the air, and in print, talking about their book, for next to nothing."

What was accomplished by the above? The teaser message is obvious: "BOOK PUBLICITY FOR AUTHORS AND PUBLISHERS solves the problem of hiring a professional publicist and shows how to get on the air, and in print, for next to nothing." The title was mentioned twice. The money button was also pushed, thus telling self-published authors that I've been there; I've fought the same battles they are fighting.

Another example:

Hostile Interviewer:

You've set yourself up as quite an authority here, Larry. Why should someone buy your book?"

Answer:

"Well, John, I've owned a public relations firm. I've been a talk show host, a reporter and publicist. I've also produced radio and television interview programs and managed a radio station."

Hostile Interviewer:

"And that makes you an expert?"

Answer:

"Now ... I'd be the last person to say that I'm the ultimate authority, but I *have spent* many years on both sides of the microphone.

"BOOK PUBLICITY FOR AUTHORS AND PUBLISHERS is based on what I've learned through years of experience. It's my bag of tricks.

"The premise is that a person doesn't have to spend $1,000 a month or more for a professional publicist.

"Everything a self-published author needs to know to get on the air is in my book."

Again, let's review what occurred. First, I didn't get into an argument. Second, the hostile question was answered totally. Third, the money button was pushed again. Fourth, the book's title was given again. Fifth, a seed was planted ... everything a self-published author needs to know to get on the air or in print is in the book.

This message must be very well thought out and delivered with a high degree of consistency and no ambiguity.

When on the air, the presentation of the topic - the teaser message - must remain consistent from station to station, publication to publication and market to market. One should be able to approach it from many angles and, in fact, should do so to keep it fresh and alive. Otherwise, there is a tendency for it to sound rote, strained and rehearsed.

For our purposes here, there are two parts to the teaser message: first the producer or editor must be sold on the concept of an interview (this will be covered in a later chapter) and, second, the message must again be sold while in the actual interview itself. Both parts of the message must be carefully thought out and should agree with each other. It wouldn't do to have a producer or editor book an interview based on one thing and then discover the guest actually wanted to talk about something else.

What should the teaser message be? One word says it all ... simple. There is an old public relations and advertising adage called K.I.S.S.: '**K**eep **I**t **S**imple,_**S**tupid.'

If the overall message is not kept simple and concise a majority of the audience can be quickly lost.

Even very complicated issues can be kept conceptually simple, hence the advice to carefully think out the message.

Probably the classic K.I.S.S. message of all time was that used by Volkswagen years ago to promote their small 'beetle' through a series of simple ads appearing in publications, on television and billboards. The ads varied, but were similar to one of the first, which showed a picture of the little car, with no words to support it other than, "Small Wonder." This series of ads exemplified the K.I.S.S. method and very clearly illustrated the concept that when it comes to a message, the less said the better. (It was one of the most successful ad campaigns ever.)

Similarly, the old Pacific Southwest Airlines (PSA) painted a simple black grin on the noses of their aircraft. Whoever saw the aircraft could not help but get the message: Happy airplanes equal happy passengers.

An author's task is to grab a potential buyer by the collar and say, "Hey! This book is the best thing since popcorn!" In print, this is primarily done through the book's cover, but it bears looking at because the overall media message must reflect the message of the book's cover.

The title to this book evolved through several different working titles as I thought how best to communicate its contents:

AIR TIME!
to:
THE MEDIA ACCESS HANDBOOK
to:
AN INSIDER'S GUIDE TO MEDIA PROMOTION
to:
MEDIA PROMOTION MADE SIMPLE
to:
The Professional Guidebook To (Almost) FREE PUBLICITY! Through Radio, TV & the Press
to:
The Author's GuideTo (Almost) FREE PUBLICITY!

Finally, we end up with a title that reflects not only the contents but the teaser message that will eventually be employed on the air and in various publications.

I've written a book for authors that will show them how to get almost free publicity through radio, television and the press. Based on my experience in the media, the book is, literally, "my bag of tricks:"

BOOK PUBLICITY FOR AUTHORS AND PUBLISHERS
- Radio
- Television

Note the progression above from air time to media access, through media promotion, to free publicity. Each title represented more clearly than the one before it the contents of this book. Why did this happen? I was fine-tuning my message, which is, simply this: "Here's the way for authors to get (almost) free publicity over radio, TV, and through the press."

The message must be clear, concise and contain a minimum amount of words.

Once an effective, yet simple, teaser message is arrived at, it must be *sold*. Don't make the mistake of forgetting that while we, as authors, have a clear understanding of our book's message or theme, others may not. The publicist and author should test the teaser message on friends to see if it communicates and adjust it if necessary before media interviews begin.

It's all a matter of *perception*. A book is really no better than the intended public perceives it to be. That's a hard fact of life, but it's the truth. An author can produce the best book the world has ever seen but if the general public perceives it to be inferior, it will most likely never sell.

It's equally important to remember that if an author should lose credibility with the public, then the game is over … at least for that particular book.

Consider also the point of view of a show's producer or a publication's editor. If an author's publicist cannot make a favorable impression, he or she is dead in the water. It's as simple as that. Members of the media are often extremely cynical. Similarly, in today's society, the general public has become cynical as well. So an author's first job, and the first job of his or her publicist, is to sell the media people on the validity of the author's book.

Conversely, if a teaser message can impress the highly cynical members of the press or of the electronic media, then it can probably impress the intended public as well. Use the media people as a sounding board (after the message has been tested on a few people at random) but *only* after it's been carefully thought out. Don't be in a hurry to rush things. Be prepared to change the message if necessary.

It helps to be aware of which stations and publications are the most popular within a given market. Approach these sources *only after* the message has been smoothed out. Save the best for last, in spite of the temptation to do it the other way around. The top rated media sources will also have the most listeners, viewers or readers. It's not a good idea to blow it with a message that doesn't communicate well.

Be truthful and <u>never</u> say anything that cannot be easily documented by credible sources.

I was once approached by a representative for a radical religious cult, who demanded that I cover a certain article the group had written regarding alleged South African suppression of his organization. As documentation, he presented the church's own in-house publication.

When I asked him questions about the article, the man grew very vague and could only point to what the article said. Obviously, he was not briefed on the issue or the basis of the article.

When I informed him that what he was giving me could not be used without further independent documentation, he became quite agitated. His instructions had been to get the story covered as news.

Again I told him I was sorry, but that I could not do it without documentation from one or more independent sources. At this point, the man literally stormed out the door.

This illustrates a very basic problem inherent to media publicity. Many people go off half-cocked and fail to back up their claims with reliable documentation.

In the case above, the group sent a person who didn't know the basis of the story and wasn't even briefed on it. His job was to get some publicity. The story might have been valid - I really don't know - but an obviously biased in-house publication simply wasn't sufficient documentation.

The publicist must be knowledgeable about the book.

An old public relations adage goes, "If you can't dazzle them with brilliance, then baffle them with b… s… !" Sadly, there are those who take this to heart and simply cannot do anything straight or truthful. They must put a kink in everything they do. Obviously this can and does create problems.

While the main idea is to get the message communicated, that does not warrant the risk of doing so in an untruthful manner. These days, there are countless numbers of investigative reporters looking to catch someone in a lie. It's much easier to simply be honest and up-front with how a message is presented. Don't oversell the book.

Credibility is often established only with difficulty.

It is also something that is easy to lose.

There is always the temptation to embellish a little. Generally speaking, there's nothing wrong with that, as long as it's kept within bounds. The line between 'dazzling them with brilliance' and 'baffling them with b … s … ' is often a fine one. This must always be kept in mind.

Credibility, once lost, can be difficult to regain.

Fortunately, there is another side to the coin. Radio stations will often re-run an exceptionally good interview, thus giving double coverage. This is very important to maintaining any sort of public contact.

Selling the Message

To gain access to free publicity, the media producers or publication editors must be sold on the validity of the book's message or topic. If that does not happen, advertising must then be created and paid for, but here again, the same rule applies - the message must be sold to the audience to be effective. If the message isn't effectively sold, if it doesn't communicate, it will quickly die.

Producers and editors receive a never-ending flow of calls and letters from people requesting an interview. Like most producers, whenever I've been involved with producing a show I first ask myself, "Does this interest me?" This is quickly followed by, "Will this interest my audience?"

While there are other criteria that I follow as well, the two preceding questions are paramount in my mind and lead to my ultimate decision to accept or reject an interview. If I feel the answer to either question is negative, I will turn the interview down. If I am confused by the request or if it is not crystal clear what the topic is, I'll likewise turn it down. End of discussion. Let them try again.

Why I would turn an interview down that did not interest me? Brilliant though the guest might be, he or she is but one half of the show. I'm the other half, and what audience I have is largely based upon their reaction to me as a show host. The people who listen to talk shows are generally pretty sharp. If they discern that the host is bored with the interview, they are likely to become bored with it as well. Also, as a producer, I'm more in tune with what my audience would like than a prospective guest will be.

This is, admittedly, a bit cold, but as the show's producer and host, I have to make value judgments. If the message is boring or not clear to me, then I must assume that the same will hold true for my audience. *This is a common attitude among media producers and publication editors !*

As a producer, I will likewise turn down any proposed interview that does not fit into my show's format. Sometimes I will refer potential guests to other producers.

I will especially turn down any potential guest who is rude, overbearing or talks down to me as the producer, as this is how that person might also act on the air. Past experience with this has all too often proven the premise true.

It's a good idea to have at least a basic idea of what a station's format is before any attempt is made to contact it and request interview air time.

Each station is built around a certain format or theme, which incorporates a general image of what management feels the station should reflect. Each format is targeted towards, and addresses, a certain segment of the population.

An overview can be as simple of knowing what sort of music, if any, the station plays (rock, jazz, classical, etc). For example, a radical concept would never work on a classical or religious station.

Knowing where to place your message can be as important as the message itself!

Be aware that a station's talk show audience might be radically different from it's music audience. Also, a given station might have several different talk shows, each with a different format and audience. The show's producer should know what will work for the show. Let the producer's interest (or lack of it) be a guideline.

Chapter 4

The Producer's Point of View

We've touched on a few of the following points earlier, but this might be a good time to review them and once again examine what producers look for when considering someone for an interview. Remember: the producer is the first person who must be sold on the concept before an interview is booked.

Throughout my years in radio, I produced my own shows, but this is not always the case. If the producer and host are separate people, it's important to remember that the producer calls the shots.

The points that follow were my criteria for determining whether to go with an interview. While other producers may have different criteria they follow, it should be noted that the following points are fairly representative of what all producers consider before booking an interview.

For purposes of clarity, the following points are presented from a dual point of view. Listed first is the *publicist's* point of view. Listed below that are the thoughts that went through my mind when I considered booking interviews. Immediately following each section will be a commentary regarding how I arrived at such criteria.

It's important for an author (and his or her publicist) to know these things if air time is being sought with any degree of regularity. But again, and at the expense of being a little redundant, remember that this list is mine; other producers might have different ideas or standards when it comes to booking their shows.

Criteria For Booking An Interview

Publicist:
What can I do or say to make this book interesting to the producer?

Producer:
Does this subject or person interest me?

I learned a long time ago to shy away from an interview if the subject or person did not interest me. Perhaps this is being too picky but we must remember that the main idea of an interview show is to not only inform but to entertain the audience as well.

An audience that is not entertained by an interview, no matter how interesting the material, will tune it out or turn it off. It must also be realized that the host of the show will attract and hold an audience based largely on the force of his or her personality.

The only time that I have relaxed this standard was when running a small, AM, community-oriented radio station in the mountains of northern California. The local paper only came out once a week and so the audience was starved for local news and information. There we had a situation where anything concerning the community interested virtually everyone. In this situation, I did many interviews that didn't particularly interest me, but were of interest to the community. If a station, especially a commercial station, wishes to remain in business, it must be responsive to the wants and needs of the community or the community segment it serves.

Publicist:
Will the book interest the producer's audience? How?

Producer:
Will the book or author interest my audience? How?

As mentioned in the paragraph above, the audience must

be kept entertained if they are to continue to listen to an interview. Only a very small percentage of the potential audience will stick with a boring interview.

Publicist:
How does this book fit into this particular show's overall theme? What can I (truthfully) say to make it more attractive to the producer?

Producer:
Does this subject fit with my show's format and purpose? How?

Every interview show has a format that is followed closely. If the show's format ever ceases to work for the station (ratings-wise) it will be changed and a better one found. For the five years I was producing at KFRC in San Francisco, my shows were well-received by the audience, and we stayed with the original format for the entire period.

In the case of the small community station (mentioned above) the format for news and features was, 'anything concerning the community at large.' For example, anything to do with local employment was well-received. Conversely, environmental issues (always good subject matter in major metropolitan areas) did not work for this show as the community based its economy primarily on the logging industry. The audience didn't want to hear about saving trees or any other subject that threatened that industry and hence their economy.

Publicist:
I must convince the producer how easy it will be to interview the author.

Producer:
Is the person I'm talking to the one who will be on the air? If so, how is this person likely to respond once in the interview?

This is a tough question to answer. The publicist might

be bright, witty and very easy to talk with, but the guest might be a clod. It remains a tough question even if the person I'm talking to is the one who will be on the air. This rule can be relaxed somewhat when dealing with an author - if the book is selling well, or shows the potential to do so, the audience will want to hear from the author.

I have yet to find an accurate method to gauge exactly how a person will react in an interview situation from just a phone call or even a personal meeting. People often do funny things when they realize the microphones are turned on and it's all for real. I can recall a number of cases where the guest reacted exactly opposite to what I had first thought. Like many other producers, I eventually just developed a gut feeling about this and would usually trust it. I was not always right, but the success rate was better than when I was simply guessing.

Like most producers and show hosts, I also developed a talent, out of necessity, for ad-libbing and carrying the guest through an interview, should the guest happen to fizzle out in the middle of the interview. It frequently happens that the guest can only talk for fifteen minutes or so and then has nothing left to say. So, in the pre-interview, I try to get a feeling for this as well.

Publicist:
Is our book controversial? Can we document any claims?

Producer:
Can this be documented - or is it hype?

Here again, a gut feeling must be trusted. Normally, someone seeking interview air time will send in a press kit that includes sample documentation of claims that are being made. Newspaper articles, endorsements from authorities and studies that have been done on the subject will all support claims being made (although these must often be taken with a grain of salt). I adapted a policy long ago of not putting anyone on the air who was making unsubstantiated claims unless it was something being presented purely for the listener's consideration. And even then, it was done with several disclaimers during the show.

In the case of an author promoting a book, this requirement can be relaxed somewhat as the interview is actually on the book itself and the audience can judge its validity and merit.

Publicist:
Is the book acceptable to the producer's audience? If not, how can I make it so?

Producer:
Is the book in good taste? Is this representative of what my audience needs to know? Is it what they want to hear?

Many producers don't believe in controversy for its own sake; but some do. Most any subject can be handled if it is carefully thought out. But here again, the question is one of good taste. I am confronted with making a judgment call. Who am I to make such a call? Well, if I am the producer and/or the host then it is, after all, <u>my</u> show. That being the case there are factors I must be aware of which the guest might never consider:

- What are the demographics of my audience?
- What have my listeners responded to, favorably and unfavorably, in the past?
- How is my audience likely to react if I put this book on the air?
- What do I know about their needs and wants?

Just because I might be interested in a certain subject does not necessarily mean that it would work for my audience. I'm not saying that I let my audience censor my show but in a way, that is what is happening. Like all producers, I must be in tune with my audience if I wish to keep them loyal. Remember the credibility issue? It applies to show hosts as well.

Publicist:
Will the producer seek opposing points of view? What might they be?

Producer:
What about opposing points of view? Will this guest be attacking anyone?

The so-called 'Fairness Doctrine' has been debated for years. Do broadcasters have the responsibility to provide opposing viewpoints or equal time for personal attacks on the air? This is a very touchy issue within the broadcast community as it deals directly with First Amendment rights.

Personally, I feel that the issue is more of a moral or ethical nature than a legal one. Responsibility comes into play here. As a broadcaster I feel that I must provide both sides of an issue. If one of my guests attacks someone on the air, then I feel that the person who was attacked has a right to present his or her side of the case as well.

If an author is promoting one cause or another, it's a good practice to objectively (and accurately) present both sides and conclude with the reasons for his or her particular stand. Rather than attack others on the air or in the press, an author can often 'take the wind out of it' by simply stating the opposing position in an honest and straight-forward fashion and the reasons for a differing viewpoint. "Senator _____ has gone on record that development of our last wild areas would be good for the economy and our nation, but I do not agree. My position is ..."

An interesting factor about this approach is that in the example above, the good senator could not claim equal air time for a personal attack, *as long as his or her position was stated honestly and accurately*. With the exception of 'shock' formats or some intentionally controversial 'news commentary' shows, no producer wants to be confronted by someone foaming at the mouth. Carry a big stick, if you must but, as Teddy Roosevelt said, "Speak softly."

Publicist:
(Usually, no way for the publicist to know.)

Producer:
Have I recently done an interview on this or a similar subject?

Most publicists soon learn it's not a good idea to try and get a particular guest on a show that has had a similar topic aired within a short period of time, usually within a month or so. If the publicist hears something or sees something similar to the topic of the book that is being promoted, then he or she should just put a note on the desk calendar to call that station in three or four month's time. That way, there's a better chance of getting on the air with an interview. Of course, if the book has a controversial topic, and only one side of the subject has been aired, the stations should be contacted with the opposing point of view.

As a producer, I've always strived for a good variety of subjects on my shows. If the subject sounds good to me and meets the criteria for my show, but I've recently done a similar interview, I'll explain this and ask to be recontacted in a few months. As a general rule, I won't schedule an interview several months in advance as too many things can happen in the ensuing time, such as schedule changes, conflicting appointments or whatever. If the author is really interested in being on my show, the publicist will work with me and follow up when I suggest.

Not every producer will pass on the reasons for not booking an interview at a particular time. When confronted with a refusal, the publicist should just take it in stride and try again in a couple of months.

Publicist:
How can I interest the producer?

Producer:
Do I really want to do an interview on this subject, or with this person?

Which brings us back to consideration number one. Do I really want to do it?

In Summary

The main point of this chapter is that the approach to media stations must be carefully thought out. Only then should the publicist begin to contact the stations, bearing in mind what is very likely going through the producer's mind. The ultimate goal is, of course, to obtain an interview booking.

The more of the producer's doubts that can be removed up front, the better the chances of obtaining an interview.

Chapter 5

Stations and Their Interview Shows

Many different formats exist in just about any area of operation: newstalk, public affairs, religious and entertainment. With that in mind, it helps to know something of the nature of the stations that will be approached, long before any attempt at actual contact is made.

Although radio is by far the most accessible medium, it would be a mistake to ignore television - standard broadcast or cable - even if televised interviews will be fewer in number.

It helps to have a working knowledge of just what is happening at each station in the chosen area of operation. The various broadcast yearbooks discussed earlier will help with news of the industry on a yearly basis. For more up-to-date information, newspapers are often a good source.

When a station moves, changes owners, changes call letters or takes over another station, the publicist should update the information in the media database.

The broadcast industry, especially radio, is volatile and subject to frequent changes. When a particular producer has changed stations it will often create new opportunities for interview bookings on *both* stations. Knowing this is good since it forces one to contact the various stations for updated information.

When calling for updated information, the publicist should talk to the station's receptionist.

The main goal is to secure an interview booking, so the only stations that have any interest for publicity purposes are those that have *locally produced* interview programs in the form of entertainment, newstalk, or public affairs. While newstalk type shows will usually generate the best response, it is generally advisable to take any booking offered.

The more people get involved with publicizing things through the media, the more they will become aware of a curious phenomenon that goes along with frequent air appearances. It seems that the phone begins to ring or letters arrive more frequently than before ... from people who never even heard the interviews!

This cumulative effect response is most likely due to three factors: the first of which has to do with raising of the consciousness level of the populace on a given subject ... the 'Hundredth Monkey Syndrome' (see glossary). Or to put it more plainly, the more something becomes known, the more response there will be to it, directly or indirectly. People will just seem to 'find' the book.

The second factor is that some people seem to love being Authorities (with a huge capitol 'A'). For example, a person might hear a show about a book dealing with the wonders of meditation, and even though he has no interest in it for himself, he will assume the authoritarian point of view and then highly recommend the book to others as just what they need to straighten out their lives.

Third, others will listen to an interview, think of a friend who would be interested, and recommend the book to them.

Both the second and third factors are examples of a second-party response.

These factors seem to work hand in hand. To bring them into play, lots and lots of coverage - interviews and reviews - is needed.

The following should be memorized and kept in mind because of the cumulative response effect (first and second-party response) that results from doing lots of interviews.

Large amounts of positive coverage, over an extended period of time will, *directly or indirectly*, **bring about an increase in sales of the book.**

Publicizing a book through the media is really not all that different from advertising, in that to get a favorable response, it's necessary to be familiar with the nature of the beast. People tend to listen to those stations that most interest them. To get an idea of a radio station's audience, listen to its programming. It can be safely assumed that the majority of conservative, middle-aged bankers, for instance, would not listen to 'heavy metal' stations. However, if they were the public someone was trying to reach, a classical, easy listening or jazz station might be the ticket. Still others might listen to country or 'oldies' stations.

However, it should be noted that a radio station might have, for example, a country music format and yet have an interview show or two on the weekends. The interview shows could very well draw a different audience than normally listened to the station. To discern the audience composition for a given show or shows, it's best to contact each station for a demographic profile.

Viewers tend to follow particular shows, and so a television station's audience demographics will vary dramatically throughout the day, whereas each radio station will attract a different listening audience or public that is fairly consistent.

LIVE TELEVISION TALK SHOWS will normally pull a good response. Again, this sort of format has the capability of capturing and holding the attention of the viewer. Compare this with the late-night public affairs program where there may or may not be much response (but go for them anyway if possible!) There's a time factor at work here. Live TV and radio talk shows are NOW.

LOCALLY-PRODUCED CABLE-TV SHOWS are extremely area-specific. They may or may not invoke much response, but don't make the mistake of ignoring them.

BROKERED STATIONS (TV and Radio) are interesting in that they will only accept programming that is paid for by the producer. There may or may not be much quality control. Here we find a proliferation of shows representing various religious, ethnic and special interest groups. Any response from the brokered station will depend upon the ability of the individual shows to garner and hold an audience. There is a potential liability in dealing with brokered stations as some of the individual producers might be less than professional. It's possible that a non-professional producer or host could very well (although not always) present topics in a most decidedly unprofessional manner and so alienate the audience to what an author has to say.

RELIGIOUS STATIONS (TV and Radio) by their very nature, are somewhat limited in the type of interviews they are willing to air. However, such stations will have a loyal audience, much the same as the newstalk stations. As such, the response from any interviews aired over them, especially for humanitarian or family issues, can be impressive.

NEWSTALK RADIO STATIONS get the most actual attention and these shows bring in the best response show for show, as their listeners are fairly loyal and a good cross-section of the general public. Generally speaking, those listening to newstalk stations are doing just that, *listening* ... the talk show is not just background noise. The newstalk audience also listens for longer periods of time than does the average audience.

Newstalk audiences can also respond immediately via telephone (and sometimes even by FAX machines) making this medium the modern version of the old town hall meeting where each person got a chance to speak his or her mind. The popularity of these stations has not escaped the notice of cable TV systems, and many have started their own call-in shows as well.

People who follow newstalk formats are generally very interested in current affairs and are hungry for information and comparative dialogue. This audience tends to respond more readily than the audience from any other sort of format. This is an important fact to remember because response is, after all, what is being sought.

MUSIC STATIONS will often offer one or more public affairs or entertainment interview shows. Much of this programming is reserved for non-profit groups. However, this is often not an absolute rule, especially when it has to do with book interviews.

Even though the response from public affairs interviews, taken on an individual basis, probably won't be overwhelming, there is the cumulative response effect of doing lots of shows to consider. The idea is to get on as many of these shows as possible.

It's simple, really. The more people who know about a given book and think positively of it, the more people who will buy it. To be successful at this sort of 'freebie' media publicity (as opposed to paid advertising) the rule should be to go after all the interviews possible. The author who accepts an interview is saying, "I'm interested in selling my book to the people who follow this station."

There is always the tendency to want to go for the big-time live TV talk shows or the major-market newstalk stations (where each show might have an audience numbering from the hundreds of thousands on up) at the expense of ignoring the smaller stations; *Do not* make the mistake of thinking less of these; and, *do not* be put off by the scheduled times that public affairs shows usually air. All positive air time is valuable.

In any major metropolitan area people are up at all hours of the night. How many people are within a fifty to one-hundred mile range of the station? Over a million? That's the potential audience. Even if three-quarters of them are sleeping during a late-night public affairs airing, that still leaves a quarter of a million people as the potential audience! Granted, they will not all be listening to one particular station at a given time, but the numbers of people who are listening can be very impressive indeed. Look at it this way ... is it worth an hour's time to reach up to 5,000 or more people? Of course it is.

NON-COMMERCIAL PUBLIC RADIO STATIONS always seem to rate highly in terms of audience response and have a solid reputation for quality programming. This is probably because they are listener-supported, much the same as with religious stations. They have extremely loyal audiences and these audiences tend to be very responsive. Most public stations will have a locally-produced interview show or two in their programming schedule and many of these shows are hosted by very capable people.

Grab all the air time possible, whenever, wherever and in whatever fashion possible!

The Grosser The Better

There's an advertising term called 'gross impression.' If one person sees one ad one time, that's one gross impression. If that same person sees the same ad twice, or if someone else sees it once, that's two gross impressions and so forth.

Typically, even a late-night public affairs interview show can garner gross impressions numbered in the thousands or tens of thousands. During the nighttime hours, especially in the lower AM frequency band, a typical 5,000 watt station can often be heard clearly as far as 300 to 500 miles away. Within a circle with a diameter of 1,000 miles, how many potential listeners would there be?

A top newstalk radio show or network TV show can provide hundreds of thousands, perhaps millions of gross impressions. By way of example, the night time broadcast footprint (area of signal coverage) of the 50,000 watt KGO AM radio in San Francisco can reach from Alaska to Mexico and inland to Idaho, Utah and Arizona, given the right atmospheric conditions.[1]

The name of the game is to garner as many favorable gross impressions as is physically possible.

---

[1] Nightime AM radio signals bounce off the inosphere, thereby dramatically extending the station's effective range.

Chapter 6

Fliers and News Releases

Several magazines exist that spotlight books and include author information, interview availability dates and such for media resources. However, even quarterly listings in these publications can be several hundred dollars. These magazines, that have national or regional distribution, are fine ... for those who can afford them. But for the author or small press owner on a limited budget who wants to reach stations or publications across the country, a simpler and less expensive alternative is needed. Fortunately, it exists: flyers and news releases.

Fliers

There's no need to produce tens of thousands of fliers. Once a master copy is in hand, fliers can be produced quite cheaply on any good copy machine. For example, consider the San Francisco/San Jose California market, that contains a little over fifty radio and TV stations. By utilizing fliers each station could be reached for not too much money and then followed up with a telephone call.

A basic low-cost flier should include a facsimile of the book cover, a page count, a basic synopsis of the book itself and a brief summation of the author's credential's. *Especially important are the dates the author will be in the individual community or if the author is available for telephone interviews.* A follow-up number is essential, in either case. Remember that if these fliers are sent to different time zones, calls could come in at weird hours.

The flier need not be multi-colored and printed on slick paper (although it helps). As in everything, one's budget will reflect the relative quality of the finished product. However, this book is not about how to produce the most expensive flier possible. It is about spending as little as is possible. With that premise in mind, consider colored paper (usually no extra charge at printers) and black ink on a standard letter-sized paper. Black on yellow is a good color for visibility.

The author should have in hand a black and white glossy of the book's cover and then have a printer screen it to be included on the flier. This could also be done by the author with an electronic scanner and laser printer if the budget allows. The fliers can then be mailed (preferably with a previous query) to the producers and editors in various markets.

Fliers can be utilized as the budget allows, especially if the author has no intention of doing out-of-state publicity tours. However, if just one good station calls for a telephone interview, or one publication decides to mention or review the book, many orders could be received.

The author's publicist should follow up on these fliers a week or so after they were sent out.

News Releases

It's easy to get wrapped up in doing radio and television interviews but forget about the press. This is a mistake and should be avoided.

Newspapers and magazines love book reviews because their readers love reading about new books and authors. The press can generate quite a bit of free publicity.

As long as a few basic guidelines are followed, there is a good possibility a news release regarding a book will get printed ... maybe not in its entirety, but printed nonetheless. Even a simple mention can be worth hundreds or thousands of dollars in free publicity and many books can be sold as a direct result.

Anything positive regarding the author or the book should be offered to the press in a news release, including the planned publication date of a new or updated version of a book.

If a book has been written on acid-rain, and an area is having problems with that, then the newspapers and magazines covering that area should all receive a news release. If the author wins a writing contest or special recognition from a certain civic group then the press should be contacted. If the author will be speaking at a civic gathering, be *live* on a local station (be sure to include the *air date and time* of pre-recorded interviews) or before a club or organization, then the press should receive a news release as well (send the release to the attention of: 'Community Events Editor'). Note that radio and TV stations will normally not promote each other's programming. Special interest magazines should also be contacted ... a magazine for dog lovers would naturally receive a news release for a book dealing with anything canine.

A good percentage of 'news' in newspapers and magazines is taken from unsolicited news releases.

Newspapers generally fall into three categories: dailies, weeklies and biweeklies. There are also sub-categories, generally based on circulation, but for our purposes here the publicist shouldn't worry about that. Sometimes the weekly or biweekly newspapers (and sometimes magazines as well) are 'throw aways,' offered for free. These are usually supported by advertising.

Magazines are usually published on a monthly basis.

News or wire services and syndicates are generally open to receiving releases. Find these listed in the broadcasting yearbooks.

Writing News Releases

News releases should be written in an inverted pyramid fashion, with the first two paragraphs containing the bulk of the information. The remaining paragraphs should provide supporting information, in a *descending* order of importance. (When editors take out their pens and begin to do the job they are paid to do, they begin at the bottom of a story and work upwards.)

The release should begin with something that will catch an editor's eye, such as statistics or a question. News of the book should be woven into current trends and events as much as possible.

The release should be written in simple language and (for everything but special-interest publications) stay away from esoteric terms and technical language. News releases should be written to be read.

Remember K.I.S.S.? It applies here as well: Keep It Simple, Stupid! The entire release should be no more than two pages.

An 'Author's Information Sheet' can be included if more information on the author is needed. This is basically a biographical sketch of the author, similar to what is found on the inside covers of some books. It need not be long and detailed. In fact, it's better if it is kept short.

A 5x7 glossy black and white photo of the author can be included if desired ... remember to make it a candid shot that relates to the content of the book if possible. One picture *is* sometimes worth a thousand words.

Just like electronic media producers, publication editors are not interested in providing free advertising for the author, but rather in providing their readers *information* that they can use. With that in mind, a local angle is important. This necessitates customizing the releases for each individual publication or area. This can easily be done on a personal computer or even a typewriter.

<pre>
                    News Release
For Immediate Release
Contact: (Publicist's Name and phone number)
</pre>

Heading

Main body of news release with paragraphs
in <u>descending</u> order of importance.

_____

_____

_____

_____

_____

_____

more …

Page Two of Two
Release Heading

Paragraphs continue if necessary -
in <u>descending</u> order of importance.

_____

_____

_____

_____

####

    The release should be written on standard letter-size paper, double spaced and with at least one or one and a quarter inch margins. The news release should be written in a basic typeface, such as Helvetica or Courier and have no typos or strike-overs.

This is Helvetica.

`This is Courier.`

Times is also good.

For news releases, avoid fancy fonts such as *Bernhard Tango: Such fonts make a release unusable.*

The words "News Release" should be centered at the top.

"For Immediate Release" tells the editors they can use the release immediately (this could also read, "For Release After [date]).

The release should be ended with '####,' '-30-,' or 'End,' all of which mean the same thing: The End.

The publicist should follow-up the news release to specific editors and ask if they would like to interview the author. This does two things: first, it forces the editor to think of one specific news release and second, even if the editor doesn't want to do an interview, it still forces him or her to concentrate, even for a moment, on one specific news release. This alone just might convince the editor to run the release or mention the book.

I personally don't believe that a publicist should ever leave a message for an editor, but not everyone agrees with me. My best recommendation is to just play it by ear and do what feels best.

As with the electronic media, the best thing to do is to persist. Postage is still cheap. The cost of printing releases and photographs is still relatively inexpensive. The only real limiting factor is the energy and drive of the publicist.

It's a numbers game.

Not all the releases a publicist sends out will get printed. But *some* will, and that's the whole idea. If only one out of 10 or 20 releases sent out gets printed, and that one in a publication that reaches, say 50,000 people or even 5,000 for that matter, the objective has been accomplished. Those that do get printed can translate directly into books being sold in great numbers.

A good indication that releases are correctly written comes when editors begin to print them verbatim.

Chapter 7

Scheduling Interviews

Upon first contacting a station or publication, the interview idea must be sold to the appropriate producer, director or editor. With this in mind, it's wise to consider thoroughly beforehand the type of book interview being proposed. Is it entertainment or more along the lines of public affairs? Is it controversial, entertaining or informational? Is it timely and, if so, will it still be valid in two or three months? (Publications and stations usually want timely material and stations, especially TV stations, sometimes schedule months in advance). All these questions must be answered before any attempt is made to sell the idea.

The producer or editor's *opinion* of the proposed interview will determine whether any coverage is offered.

It's natural to make a few mistakes early on. There may even be some negative response to the interview idea. If this happens, don't despair, just keep on calling different stations and publications. A particular station or publication can always be tried again in a month or so. It may be easier to schedule an interview at that time, due to the book becoming more timely, a new producer has arrived at the station or whatever. Conditions, opinions, people and interest, can and do, change.

When met with a negative response, the publicist should politely ask why the producer is not interested. If a number of producers or editors express the same reasons it may indicate that the suggested interview needs to be reconsidered and the topic approached from a different angle. This could also indicate that current events do not mesh with the book's topic.

Both the author and publicist should keep an eye on news trends. It's beneficial to work in harmony with them whenever possible. News is a cyclical thing and topics come in and out of 'vogue' all the time. Being aware of these trends can help with extra bookings.

Don't be picky about interview bookings ... they are *all* potentially valuable.

One of my clients was once offered a six-minute noon news interview on a television station almost a hundred miles distant. We discussed the relative merits of doing the show, as practically an entire day would be consumed in going to do it. In spite of a rather busy schedule he finally agreed to the interview and, together, we left at 9:00 in the morning to drive to the station. We arrived, did the interview and were on the road back to his office by 12:30 p.m. We arrived there just after 2:45 p.m..

Immediately after my client's segment had aired (about 12:20 p.m.) his office phones had begun to light up. In the ensuing two hours and twenty-five minutes over 60 inquiries had been made for his services. The calls continued to come in the rest of the day.

More inquiries were received within the next two days; eventually they totalled over 130; Not bad for one day spent on the road and six minutes in an interview!

Newspapers present a somewhat different aspect. But, just as in lining up a radio or TV interview, the same rules apply. The publicist should follow-up the press release, and without being overbearing, attempt to line up an interview with the book review editor. (Any editor can review a book, but the publicist should attempt to tag an interview onto the book review.)

Be aware that magazines are sometimes laid out months in advance and the book review editors might want an advance copy of the book to time their review with it's release. Any magazine interview or review will usually appear months down the road.

Whenever doing such interviews, the author should be aware of the time factor involved and speak from that perspective; interviews for magazines should be time-less whenever possible.

There really isn't a lot of magic involved in being a good publicist. Work, yes, but not magic. That I have been successful in this area is largely the result of two main factors. The first of these is that, over the years, I came to a good understanding of the electronic media game (especially radio). In no small part, this understanding included the way producers think. The second factor is that my techniques were developed on a trial and error basis over the years into a simple and proven method for lining up publicity.

The publicist must remember to smile into the telephone. There is no need to be cute or clever or to play mind games, primarily because a straightforward approach work's best. Media people really aren't that much different from anyone else in that they respond positively to open and honest communication. In fact, most of them, especially in radio, are pretty nice people to work with ... a little nuts at times, but good people.

Contacting The Stations

When first contacting a station, the publicist should be prepared to relate the interview suggestion to known community problems, to the news of the day (if applicable) or to just the way the interview will capture and hold an audience's attention. When the producer is on the line, the publicist should dive right in and go for it. *At best*, the publicist will have a minute or two to sell the concept of the interview.

Let's create a typical situation wherein a publicist, say from Sunset Hill Publications, is calling a station to line up some air time for a new Sunset Hill book. This is a cold call, where the publicist does not yet have a contact at the station.

Note that once the publicist has the full attention of the producer, she simply dives right into the presentation of her message to the producer, but is not over-bearing or rude about it. If the producer were to interrupt the publicist and say she didn't have time to talk at the moment, the publicist would simply acknowledge that and politely ask when would be a better time to call back. The first question is to the station's receptionist:

Publicist: "Hello, who handles your interview programs?"

Receptionist: "That would be Laurie Johnson. May I say who's calling?"

Publicist: "This is Deborah Lynn with Sunset Hill Publications."

Receptionist: "One moment and I'll connect you."

(PUBLICIST WRITES DOWN 'LAURIE JOHNSON')

Producer: "Hi, this is Laurie."

Publicist: "Hello Ms. Johnson, my name is Deborah Lynn and I'm with Sunset Hill Publications. I'm calling about the new release from one of our authors, J.D. Sebastion. Do you have a moment to talk about it?"

Producer: "Just barely. I've got to run to an interview in a few minutes. What's the topic of the book?"

Publicist: "The book we've just published by Mr. Sebastion is called 'Saving Lives, Saving Limbs.' The subject is emergency field first aid. The book is written for hunters, hikers, campers and fishermen; in short, anyone who enjoys the outdoors.

"Mr. Sebastion recently retired after twenty years in the army as a field medic, and currently works as a hunting and fishing guide in Alaska, so he certainly has the proper credentials.

"Not only is he knowledgeable, but he's funny as well and gives a good interview. If possible, we'd like to schedule an appearance on one of your interview programs."

Producer: "I've often wondered when someone was going to do a book on that. It's certainly needed! I can think of any number of occasions when my husband and I were hiking that we could have used that book. Are you local or on tour?"

Publicist: "Mr. Sebastion will be in your area the week of March 20th. Is there any way we can schedule an interview during that week?"

Producer: "Well, you've certainly given me enough lead time. I would like to see a press kit, the book or a flyer before I decide though. If you could send me something I would appreciate it."

Publicist: "I'm glad to do it! I'll get a copy of 'Saving Lives, Saving Limbs' and some information in the express mail today. I'll touch bases with you again in a week or so to make sure you got it. The 'Saving Lives, Saving Limbs' book and packet will be in a bright yellow envelope, so you won't have trouble seeing them. Is the station still located at 4538 West Tompkins?"

Producer: "Yes it is. I'll be looking for your material. It sounds interesting."

Publicist: "Thank you. I'll get the material off and then talk to you again in a week or so. Have a good day!"

Producer: "Thank you. Good bye."

This conversation is fairly typical of a first call. Of course if the producer was known, it would be less formal, but the same rules would apply.

Let's review what occurred in the above example:

> 1) The publicist was cheerful, brief and to the point. Rather than take the producer's time for granted, the publicist asked the producer if there was a moment to discuss a prospective interview. This did two things: it showed respect for the producer's time and it opened the dialog on a safe area.
>
> 2) The publicist did not attempt to play mind games with the producer.
>
> 3) The publicist got the idea across ("Here's a useful book that will help people with emergency medical care in the field.") but she didn't force it on the producer.
>
> 4) The publicist twice expressed a desire for an interview and gave the producer a good amount of lead time to decide. (For a publicity tour in which the author planned to be in the producer's city in March, the publicist would have called about the last week of January.)
>
> 5) The producer requested that some information be sent for review and consideration.
>
> 6) The publicist agreed to send the information, and alerted the producer that the press kit would be bright yellow.
>
> 7) The publicist confirmed the station's address.

8) The publicist told the producer twice to expect follow-up call.

9) The publicist mentioned the name of the book three times and the author's name four times. (When the bright yellow packet arrived at the station, it would *not* be just another submission.)

Very seldom is an interview booked on the first call, unless the person to be interviewed is a celebrity. It's best to call three to four weeks ahead for a local show. When booking for a publicity tour, six to eight weeks lead time is usually sufficient. Television shows, especially those on the network, are sometimes booked up months in advance.

Since a 3x5 media card will have already been made up for the station, the publicist would pencil in the name of the person responsible for the interviews. If the address is different, it would be changed on the card <u>and</u> in the broadcasting yearbook. (It's best to make all changes in pencil.)

Next, the publicist would take a letter- or legal-size sheet of ruled paper (it doesn't matter which, just as long as it is consistent and matches the manila file folders) and on the top of the paper, list the station's call letters, address and phone number. The station's frequency would be listed (i.e. KFRC AM 610). The publicist would then date the first line and on it, list the name of the person talked to, the outcome of the call (booking, send info, etc.) and the date for follow-up (usually 7-10 days hence) or further action. That is the start of a data sheet. It's this sheet and the media cards that form the bulk of the media database:

```
1/18/92 - Spoke with Laurie Johnson. She
said she wondered when someone would write
a book on the subject of emergency first-
aid in the field. She sounded quite
interested and said she hikes often with
her husband. Send info and follow-up by
```

<u>Feb. 1 for a March interview while on tour in Spokane</u>

The publicist would then file the data sheet in the appropriate folder. A note would be attached to the folder reminding her to send the packet of information to the station. The folder would then be placed aside for later action.

The publicist would continue to contact other stations or media sources and repeat the same process for each station contacted. If she received an absolute negative reply, she would note this on the data sheet for that particular station, place the sheet in the appropriate manila folder and then file it away ... the media card for that station would be marked appropriately (i.e. '1/18/21-no interview shows.') Note that this station would be followed up again in two or three month's time ... at that point, it might have an interview show. The same would happen if the producer simply had no interest on the first call.

If the proper person could not be reached at a given station, the publicist would simply note this information on the data sheet and fix a note to file folder as a reminder to call again. (It's not a good idea to leave a message for station personnel to call back. It's up to the author or publicist to reach them, not the other way around.) Trying to reach someone time and again when they are not in is a waste of time. It's best to inquire about the ideal time to reach the contact.

The folders for stations that the publicist could not reach the producer would be sat aside and tried later. The folders for the stations that did not have interview shows would be filed away. The folders for the stations that requested information would be put in a separate file for action later that day or the next.

The publicist would then ensure she had the correct postage and send the appropriate information and materials to the station, with a cover letter included. (Note: For all local operations, regular mail service is fine. When a publicity tour is being set up [more on this later] use express mail or an express freight company such as UPS or Federal Express.)

The next entry on the data sheet would read:

```
1/18/92 - Sent press kit and book. Follow-
up by Feb. 1
```

The publicist's next action would be to turn the desk calendar to the appropriate date and write a reminder to call the station. (Note: any interview schedulings would also be noted on the desk calendar, on the data sheets and on the wall calendar!)

When the appropriate day showed up on the desk calendar, the publicist would see her note to call the station. She'd pull the station's media file, scan the data sheet to bring her up to speed on what had previously transpired and then place the call. With any luck at all, she'd line up an interview.

It's that easy.

These actions would be repeated, time and again until each targeted media source within a given area had been contacted.

I've found that it's best to contact station personnel between the hours of 10:00 a.m. to noon, and then from 1:00 p.m. until 4:00 p.m. or so, and then begin putting the press kits and letters together for mailing. Or, a day can be spent calling and then everything mailed out the next day … but the publicist should be careful about putting things off, as things can and do happen to throw off the best of intentions.

Newspaper editors are best contacted in the mornings for those papers that come out each afternoon. For newspapers that come out in the mornings, try contacting the editors after lunch. When in doubt about a weekly or bi-weekly newspaper's deadline, ask or check their publication day … their deadline will likely be sometime the previous day. Note that the best time to contact newspaper editors is *not* anywhere near their deadline!

Remember that formats and personnel can and do change and that topics that held little interest yesterday might suddenly become 'hot' tomorrow due to breaking news stories. Conversely, there is nothing colder to a station's program director than yesterday's news. Some topics remain in vogue for weeks or even months, yet others quickly drop from sight as they are replaced by ' hotter' topics.

The most important steps here are to:

- Note the person's name on the card - make certain of the correct spelling.

- The personal touch is best. Note anything of interest about the producer or editor. When the follow-up call is made, the call can be personalized. It's surprising how simple statements such as, "How's your new baby?" can open doors to interviews.

- List the publication name or call letters and follow-up date on a desk calender,

- Attach a note to the media file as a reminder to send out the information.

- Send out the information with a cover letter.

- Follow-up on the appropriate day. Normally, a week to ten days is sufficient for the station to get the information and for the producer to go over it, so the follow-up date should be planned accordingly. Be sure to note the proper call letters or publication name on the planning calender as well!

- Note on the data sheet any action taken regarding that particular station or publication, including interviews completed, 'thank you' notes sent out, etc. Now that this first bit of information is on the data sheet, it can be reviewed at any time and will indicate just what transpired; who was spoken to; what was said; what action was taken.

- Note any booking dates on the data sheet, the desk calendar and on the wall calendar.

Submissions - The Press Kit

The press kit should be carefully thought out. It must be complete, but not burdensome or redundant.

The publicist should have a cover letter already made up that can be personalized to individual stations and publications. If it's not stored in a computer where it can be instantly recalled, have a master letter to work from. (Don't just send form letters as they are in bad taste and impersonal - the idea is not to turn producers and editors off but to catch their attention.)

The typewritten cover letter should:

- be professional and to the point,

- be written on letterhead stationary,

- thank the person for his or her time on the telephone and reintroduce the request for air time,

- include a brief summation of the proposed topic and indicate a return telephone number,

- be no more than one page long,

- should go with a press kit that includes:

    ... a brochure, flyer, or the actual book. (Note: It's not necessary for each station or publication to receive a copy of the book. But, for any major media source it might be a good idea to send one.),

... a sample of any press clippings available, other supporting documentation (don't get too carried away here; most producers are overloaded with information that they don't have time to read),

... a list of fifteen or twenty suggested interview questions,

... (Note - this is optional) a 5x7 inch glossy black and white *candid* photo of the author and

... a biography sheet on the author.

There is an advertising term called 'noise' or sometimes, 'clutter.' What the terms refer to is the combined information being presented to the public from other advertising sources that reduces or completely obscures the clarity or receipt of a message. The trick for an advertiser is to somehow overcome the competition's noise so that the public pays attention to his particular product.

Because a major station can easily receive fifty to seventy-five or more books a week, all from authors seeking interviews, the use of brightly-colored, glossy folders helps reduce the 'noise.' Any bright, fluorescent color will work well. (Bright yellow is a great stand-out color. The idea is to send one that stands out from the rest.)[1]

An option would be to acquire a bright presentation folder for the press kit and then mail the folder inside a sealed clear plastic wrap. Home food sealing machines are good for this purpose. Self-adhesive 5x7 inch labels can be stuck on the plastic for the address, return address and postage.

When setting up a publicity tour, a list of the days when the author will be in that station's city should also be included

---

[1] Quality Park Products (2520 Como Ave., St. Paul, MN 55108 – 1-800-637-5770) puts out a fine line of brightly-colored envelopes in red, yellow, green, orange and blue. Call for sizes, prices or the location of their nearest dealer.

in the press kit. This is all stuffed into the brightly colored, glossy, two-pocket folder mentioned above. It is easy to get carried away here, but the idea is to have the author's press kit stick out from the rest. Inquiries usually end up in a pile on a desk, so it helps if the producer or editor knows to look for a brightly-colored folder.

The publicist should make it a point to religiously update the desk calendar daily.

Keeping the media files straight and up to date is vital. The importance is one of knowing exactly what has previously transpired or what was said. A last notation, "Follow-up sometime this fall," is a reminder to do just that. This would also have been noted on the desk calendar, probably sometime around the middle of October of the beginning of November. At that time, seeing the notation to call on the daily calendar, the proper file would be pulled and reviewed as to the reason for the notation and a call would be made.

The importance of having the media files and keeping them current, cannot be overstated. Without some indication of what previously transpired, a publicist is just shooting in the dark.

Like a bank book, the desk calendar should always 'balance' at the end of the work day.

For each scheduled call or action that was completed, there should be a notation on the individual media file to confirm that.

For each call that needed to be rescheduled, there should be a notation on the appropriate day on the desk calendar.

For each information packet or letter which needed to be sent, there should be a packet ready to mail out, and the appropriate notations placed on the individual media cards.

A line should be drawn through each calendar note as it is completed.

The publicist should check the desk calendar first thing in the morning, several times throughout the day and just before quitting work.

The publicist should check, check, and then recheck. The publicist should KNOW what actions need to be done. It is also helpful to do one thing, *and only one thing* at a time.

The Daily Grind

The cycle of contacting stations and making the proper notations as to what happened (outlined above) should be repeated for every station in the proposed area of operation.

The above is an on-going, daily operation but it really isn't necessary to contact everyone at once.

Contacting or following up five or six stations a day will keep a person busy.

When the interviews begin to happen, the author and publicist might become too busy for the publicist to make calls each day. He or she might even go a week or so without contacting anyone.

The rule is to keep doing it and not slack off and expect the media producers or print editors to return calls.

A good habit for the publicist to get into is to send a confirming note to each station the day that an interview booking is set up. The note should be simple and short, but always briefly restate the topic and the name of the author. It should also include the publicist's name and telephone number.

The publicist should confirm the interview again by telephone a day before the interview is scheduled.

A Few Words On Stress

Under stress, which just seems to go hand-in-hand with the publicist's job, most of us succumb (sooner or later) to a condition laughingly - but accurately - called 'CRN' or "Can't Remember Nuthin'!"

When stress begins building up, it just seems that brain fade is common. But if the publicist has taken the time to note something on the calendar, he or she can avoid the embarrassment of fading out or making a mistake.

Take a tip from someone who has fought the same battles and emerged, if a little beat up and battered, somewhat wiser for the experience.

Let the actions described here become automatic and they will go a long ways towards reducing stress. There's no need for the publicist to be a martyr ... the job should be fun.

Another note on stress ... not speaking as a nutritionist, but more as one who has fought the battle ... it's well known that stress drives vitamin B and other essential vitamins and minerals from our bodies. Keeping the proper fuel in our system goes a long ways towards holding the stress level down.

I've found that the micro-algae spirulina is a particularly excellent source of vitamins, iron, beta-carotene, minerals and amino acids. The beautiful thing about spirulina is that it has the ability to detoxify and energize one's body and satisfy hunger without bringing on the jangles of artificial stimulants such as caffeine, sugar or drugs. It's a pure food source and one just feels more alert and has more energy while taking it.

My first introduction to spirulina came as the result of an interview I conducted at KFRC years ago. Since then, I've become a devotee of it.

Rochester

In America, spirulina is sold as a food supplement and is available at most drug stores and many super-markets. As a general rule, though, the best spirulina is found at natural-food stores or through speciality distributors.[1]

Just as in driving, one should not attempt to do interviews while under the influence of drugs or alcohol. Similarly, it's not a good idea to attempt to interviews after eating a particularly heavy meal (more on this later). It goes without saying that the author should be alert and ready for the interview. The ingestion of any substance or food that will slow one down should be avoided.

Good nutrition is the key, for both the author and the publicist. The author must be 'on' and ready for the interview ... the same rule applies to the publicist when contracting anyone in the media. The publicist and the author should both remember that media people have made their careers on their ability 'to read' others and then pass their observations on.

---

[1] The best source of spirulina and associated products that I've found to date comes from the Light Force® Company. Contact Dee Gretzler at Box 701, San Bruno, CA 94066 or Box 2445, Oroville, CA 95965 for information and prices.

Chapter 8

The Follow-Up Call

Once the materials have been sent, out a follow-up should not be attempted sooner than a week to ten calendar days hence.

Station producers need time to go over any materials they receive. Early follow-up will only waste time, so the publicist should be patient and give the system time to work.

Follow-up calls should be made according to the schedule previously laid out on the desk calender. If, for some reason, the follow-up call is not made or the appropriate person reached, the original reminder should be crossed out and another call scheduled on the desk calender for later in the day or the next working day.

Occasionally, a call may need to be rescheduled many times. It will make the job a lot easier if calls are automatically rescheduled when necessary. As calls get completed or rescheduled, they should be crossed off the calendar.

It helps to pull the appropriate files needed for each day's calls before the day's work is begun. This serves to do a couple of things: first, they are on the desk and serve as a constant reminder that the calls must be made; second, each individual file is readily at hand when the call is made to that particular station or publication.

When contact with the producer is made, the publicist should remind the producer that, when last spoken to, the producer requested that a press kit be sent. The publicist should ask if the kit has arrived and if the producer has had a chance to go over it.

If the kit hasn't yet arrived, or if it has arrived and the producer hasn't had a chance to go over it, the publicist should *cheerfully* acknowledge that and promise to call later.

The above information should be noted in the appropriate media file, and if needed on the desk calendar.

It's important that the publicist be patient, courteous and work with the producers.

The publicist should not take it personally if trouble is experienced getting through to the producer, as media people are quite often running around the station at nothing less than warp speed. As mentioned in the previous chapter, it's not a very successful action to ask producers to return calls, for it is the responsibility of the person who is seeking an interview to reach the producer and not the other way around. Because of the necessity for person-to-person communication, leaving a message just won't cut it. The publicist should just be patient and try again - as many times as it takes.

> I can recall any number of instances where I pursued a given station for months on end to no avail. Then, as if by magic, an interview booking was secured. Similarly, a call would come out of the blue from a station, looking for one of my clients.
>
> One such call came the day before Thanksgiving for a booking over one of the top newstalk stations in the country. Reluctantly, the client agreed to cut his Thanksgiving dinner short do the show. As a result, several hundred inquires were made for his services and products within the next couple of weeks.

Once the producer has gone over the press kit, he or she may want to book an interview at that time, talk to the director, or think it over.

It must be noted that, when a station receives a press kit and isn't immediately interested in booking an interview, the information just might be filed away for future consideration.

Many producers will watch news trends and try to have their shows reflect current events whenever possible. When the producer decides to do a show or series of shows on a certain topic, these old press kits will be dug out of the files and given a second look.

The goal is to schedule an interview, so the publicist should do this if at all possible. However, it should be noted that any station worth its salt is constantly bombarded with interview requests and there just might have to be a wait.

Many producers schedule shows weeks or even months in advance (for the bigger shows) and this can be frustrating at times.

If there is a time element involved (i.e. if the author will only be available for interviews on certain dates) the producer should have been alerted to that in the interview proposal. It never hurts to go over this fact again in the follow-up call.

If the producer agrees to an interview and gives a time and a date but there is some uncertainty that the author can make it, the publicist should ask if the interview can be tentatively scheduled.

The publicist should confirm a tentative interview the next day or by a certain agreed upon date. Normally, producers will not have a problem with this, just as long as the publicist *doesn't forget to call them back with a definite yes or no.*

If a conflict exists with the author's schedule, the publicist should ask for an alternate date and time.

The publicist should keep in mind that at this point, the author and the book has captured the interest of the producer and are considered valuable commodities to the station.

Short of lying, the publicist should do whatever is necessary to book an interview.

If a particular show is done live at 6:00 a.m. on Sunday mornings, at 11:00 p.m., or even at 2:00 a.m., the publicist should schedule it and make certain the author shows up on time, bright-eyed, bushy-tailed and ready to do the interview.

Until one becomes a celebrity author it's a grave mistake to refuse to go the extra distance required to do these shows.

Remember: *no air time is wasted* and, with very few exceptions, an interview, regardless of when it airs, is better than no interview!

The publicist should not *under any circumstances* get on the producer's case for a better taping time, air date or anything else!

While it is true that the station now desires an interview, the fact remains that the author needs the interview more than the station does. The publicist and author should always keep that in mind.

The main idea is for the publicist to work with the producers, send out whatever additional information they may require or whatever else is needed and then show up with the author when the producer requests.

The station has the option of canceling or rescheduling the interview at any time. If this happens, the publicist and author should simply take it in stride and ask for another date, or inquire as to the best time to recontact the producer.

The publicist should note everything down in the media file plus make any appropriate notations on the desk calendar and on the master wall calendar.

The publicist and author should *never, ever* flatly turn down an interview opportunity.

With advertising air time costing sometimes in excess of $300.00 per half-minute on radio and often more than double or triple that on television, it just makes good sense to take whatever time the stations are willing to grant.

Appearing on radio or television is a privilege granted by

the station and not a right. The publicist and author shouldn't abuse that privilege by being picky about interview taping or air times because picky people sometimes find it impossible to get any air time at all.

On the follow-up call, the producer may have to be resold on the idea of the interview, why the author would be good for his or her particular show. (This is where homework pays off - it is very helpful to know about a show's format.) The publicist should be polite and, especially important, not say *anything* that cannot be documented.

Many times, when trying to get various clients on the air, I was hit with skepticism by a station producer regarding the prospective interview (especially when promoting a controversial subject). I handled this successfully, more often than not, by simply stating that I would probably be skeptical as well if our roles were reversed, but that I would be glad to furnish any documentation they desired. That would normally defuse the situation sufficiently to allow the producer to at least listen to what I had to say. Often, an interview would be scheduled.

The idea is not to get into an argument, but rather to use a little friendly persuasion.

If a particular producer simply has no interest, then he or she should not be pushed. Another attempt can always be made in a few months. Perhaps the station has another show that an interview on the book might better fit into. Again, the publicist should write everything down.

What we are dealing with here is simply a number's game. A number of stations and producers have to be contacted to generate a successful media publicity campaign.

To achieve a good share of the potential audience or readers, the media sources must present interesting people, stories and programming. They must also stick to a well-defined format, be professional, responsive to public demands and consistent in their delivery.

Above all, a media source must broadcast or print what the majority of its public wants to hear or see. The various editors, producers, show hosts and columnists are aware of these factors. This is a fact that the publicist and author must live with and never lose sight of.

If turned down by a producer or editor, the author or publicist should not take it personally. It's important to never upset anyone at the various stations or publications. Don't make enemies and don't make waves ... just take it in stride when turned down. Be professional and polite. The station can always be approached again in a few months.

It's common to be calling a station and come across someone who previously turned the interview down at their previous station. Now, with this new station, the topic being proposed for an interview might fit in perfectly with one show or another and an interview can be scheduled.

It can also work in reverse.

The publicist might come across a producer who previously booked an interview with the author at another station. *If the experience for the producer was a pleasant one*, it might be possible to book an interview on this new station.

That also clears the way for calling the producer's last station and talking to the new producer there. The publicist should stay on his or her toes and take the initiative when things like this happen.

Of course, in either case above, if the previous experience was not pleasant and left a bad memory, well ... the importance of being polite and professional is obvious.

Chapter 9

The Art Of Being Interviewed

There's an art to it, being a good interview subject. This is especially true whenever the author is confronted with a show host who just isn't up to par, at which point the author must supply the impetus for the interview. I'm not sure if this art can be taught, but what I'll attempt here is to merely include a few observations regarding interviews.

As mentioned previously, the actual interview consists of a giving and a taking, wherein the host or hostess 'gives' the show to the guest and then 'takes' it back. This giving and taking should, in an ideal situation, fall into a natural rhythm with no awkward pauses and without the guest and host speaking over each other.

While it is up to the host to set the timing, this will not always be the case, as some hosts simply play off their guests and follow, rather than lead them.

Without being intrusive, the author just might have to force the give and take; finesse is what is required.

It goes without saying that someone who has mastered the art of being interviewed will apply it in such as fashion that it looks easy.

The basics of studio etiquette, dress and composure will, of course, have been mastered long ago and now just taken as a given. The author will feel at ease talking about his or her book on the air and be able to approach the topic from any angle.

I'm reminded of an ancient Zen story.

It seems that one day an old Zen master was walking

along a road, carrying a heavy sack on his back. He was confronted by a man who demanded to know the meaning of enlightenment. Without a word, the old master unshouldered his burden and set it away from him.

"Ah, I see," said his challenger, after a period of time, "But what is there after enlightenment?"

In answer, the old Zen master shouldered his burden once again and continued on his way in silence. His challenger, seeing the truth in this, became enlightened.

Even the most knowledgeable of us must keep in mind and apply the basics, mainly because they will always have to be done. Whether by beginner or master; the burden will still have to be carried.

When being interviewed, knowing what to do is equally important as the application of what one knows. No matter how expert the author is or has become, there is still the interview at hand to contend with.

The master artisan must take the same steps as the novice, but being the master, the steps have become second nature to him and are done without thought.

Of course, the master makes it look deceptively easy and quite natural ... sometimes.

>It was to be my last show in San Francisco before leaving for the mountains of northern California to assume management of a radio station.
>
>For five years I had been interviewing people over KFRC. That's an awfully long time to be interviewing people but not to have the experience of *being interviewed*.
>
>My co-host, Robin, who would be inheriting the show when I left, thought that this would be an ideal time for the audience to get to know me as the subject of an interview and introduce her as the permanent host.
>
>This seemed a good idea so I agreed and looked forward

to being interviewed by Robin. Little did I know I was about to learn a lesson in humility.

Just before we started taping, I found myself going through all the symptoms of a nervous interview subject. Robin was in the driver's seat and I sat on the opposite side of the console, where my guests usually sat. Nothing seemed right. It didn't occur to me at first that I was seeing the studio from the opposite angle and was disoriented because of it.

I wondered if this was what my guests often felt. I didn't know, but I suddenly got mike fright and we had to do the opening of the show a couple of times before I calmed down. It was several minutes before I remembered how to be a good interview subject. Finally, I relaxed, centered myself and had fun with the interview.

Before actually being interviewed, it might be a good idea for the author and the publicist to begin listening to talk shows on radio and TV, paying special attention to the really good guests and what they are doing that makes them come across.

One thing becomes immediately apparent about people who have mastered the art of being interviewed: they tend to speak in everyday language, avoiding technical terms or an esoteric language whenever possible.

It substantially detracts from the interview when a guest will answer a question posed by the host and then proceed to explain his answer - especially in lengthy terms.

When being interviewed for radio, television or the press, the author is communicating certain realities, imparting information about his or her book. The trick is to impart the reality of the book in such a manner that the audience will respond favorably, take the information and make it their own. There is also the importance of being consistent, because people may hear an interview with the author over several different stations and read about the book or the author in a publication or two.

The temptation to experiment, to change the message somewhat, is always present but care must be taken to not change the central theme. If the message is changed too often, the audience or readers cannot help but wonder what is going on.

The author who has the ability to bring his or her topic down out of the ozone and into the living rooms of the listening audience will be miles ahead of the game. This is where talking *to* the audience and the host rather than *at* them comes into play. Talking *to* the audience implies a direct one to one communication. The result is that each member of the audience gets the feeling the speaker was talking directly to him or her. Talking *at* the audience implies more of a shotgun approach.

Talking to the audience, as opposed to talking at it is a subject I've given a lot of thought to. To say that it's important, even essential, for an author to master this art, would be a gross understatement. But, how to teach it?

In retrospect, those I've interviewed who have mastered this art seem to direct the conversation towards an *understanding* on the part of the audience through the copious use of examples. Similarly, they tend to personalize interview answers. Instead of saying, "My theory indicates that ..." they'll say, "People will find their lives easier if they..."

Rather than try to *describe* what it is that the author writes about, he or she should try to involve the audience in the *experience* of it; get them to *feel* what is being talked about.

The problem with many interview guests is that they give interesting but dry, and far too short, answers to questions posed by the show host. Often, the answer almost restates the lead-in question. Very little real dialog is involved. As a result, there is little to interest the audience.

People have a *need* to know details, to be *close* to the action. When colorful details are provided by an author, the audience tends to get caught up in the interview and many will seek out the book to see what else it contains. It's far better to *involve* the audience than it is to leave them hanging.

Without getting bogged down in details, the author should deliver a basic, but complete concept of his or her book within the allotted time of the interview. Along this same line, the author should make each interview answer a complete story, in and of itself, aware of the fact that many audience members will not hear or see the entire interview.

A good rule to remember in publicity (or advertising) is to reach out to *two* primary publics: those who are *immediately* interested and those who could be *convinced* to be interested, hence the rule for keeping the audience entertained. Initially, these are two totally separate audiences. With this in mind, the author should approach the interview accordingly.

Remember that a 30-minute interview does not mean the guest will be talking for 30 minutes. The author should be aware of this fact and pace his or her answers, as opposed to trying to take up the entire show with one question and one answer.

When being interviewed, there is a time to talk and a time to shut up and listen. Mostly, it's just common courtesy and common sense.

The show host will usually cut a guest off if he or she is getting too long winded, if it is time for a station or commercial break or if the guest begins to ramble. This is where being brief and to the point with an answer to the host's questions comes into play. A guest naturally doesn't want to cut his or her answers short. It's just human nature to want to elaborate but the necessity is also one of being brief.

What must be attained is a balance between brief answers and details.

It's better to run out of things to say and have to ad-lib than it is to hit the end of the show in the middle of an explanation and not get to finish it. Because the attention span of the listening audience really isn't all that great, this necessitates short, but complete, answers.

When doing a radio interview, it might be a good idea for the author to occasionally glance at his or her watch and see how much time is remaining, as time tends to fly by in the actual interview.

When being interviewed, the author should be prepared for anything.

As mentioned earlier, talk show hosts will often more or less ask the same basic questions. The trick is to not be lulled by this, as one never really never knows what a show host is going to ask. This is especially important on live call-in talk shows, where callers sometimes ask the dumbest questions. It's a good idea to expect the producer to have a mixture of pro and con calls lined up.

Just as one never knows what a show host is going to ask, it's also true that one never knows what they will do when on the air.

When being interviewed, it's usually very difficult to get a good feeling for how the interview is going, as attention is on answering the questions posed by the host or the callers. The show's host is very much aware of the pace of the interview and will do anything possible to keep it moving along.

No show host wants an interview that drags. Lively, spirited interviews are the ideal.

> As a show host, I'm very much aware of the interview as it progresses. A part of me, an 'observer,' somewhere off in another space-time, is hearing the interview as if he were sitting down and listening to it on the radio at home. From this distant perspective, he can discern whether the show needs to be speeded up, slowed down, made more serious, lightened up a little or perhaps controlled slightly better. This 'observer' then communicates to me what to do.

Over the years, all talk show hosts develop several tricks for adjusting the interview speed as they go along and implement these as needed. Neither the guest nor the audience is aware of the adjustments, although they will usually be spotted by other talk show hosts. The guest and the audience just perceive that the interview went like clockwork.

Most show hosts will be professional in every manner, but not all. With this in mind, the author should arrive for an interview prepared to talk the entire length of it, as opposed to making one or two brief statements and then running out of things to say.

It may sound strange to consider this, but many guests actually show up for interviews with little or (horror of horrors) *nothing* to say! From the perspective of the show host, this is extremely unnerving. First of all, it has the capability of ruining the interview and, second, the guest comes across looking like a complete idiot.

Authors should be up to date on whatever is happening in their field of endeavor. When publicizing a controversial book, authors should be well-versed on the message of the opposition and be able to objectively present it as well as their own.

In these days of libel suits for any slight, real or imagined, authors must also be careful. It's sometimes better to not mention people or organizations by name. "Some people in our field feel that ...," is much safer than, "Belchfire Motors, has taken the stand that ..."

If the host of the show mentions the opposition and asks the author to comment, the author would be well advised to preface his or her comment with, "Well, I can't pretend to speak for Belchfire Motors, but I feel that ..." or, "The president of Belchfire Motors is on record stating that, ' ... ' My perspective is different. I feel that ..."

No small part of the art of being interviewed is the ability to remain calm and objective under any sort of pressure. A show's guest can get a lot more mileage out of being objective, as opposed to foaming at the mouth. Audiences respond positively to genuine objectivity, as in the example above.

Without becoming pompous or overbearing, the author should never lose sight of the fact that he or she is being presented as an authority and should carry that fact with an air of calm assurance.

Sitting at home, listening to or watching an interview, it all seems so calm and easy. But, it's not always that way. This is especially true on television shows. The viewing audience is usually not aware of people running around shifting cameras, signalling the host, adjusting lights and so forth. Most often, television interviews are conducted on very small sets in rooms or on sound stages which might be as big as a basketball court.

As stated previously, people in the interview must create their own little world, regardless of the space and movement around them, and then conduct the interview from within that space.

It's much the same sometimes on radio. The host might have to do the show without an engineer or producer and be forced to contend with cueing up and starting commercials, doing station breaks, adjusting the microphones and such, while the interview is in progress. The host might ask a question and get out of the chair to go do something on the other side of the room or even leave the room while the guest is answering.

In both of the above instances, the guest must suffer through this as if nothing untoward is occurring. The guest must *be there, in the interview*, centered and not distracted or thrown off by anything. The necessity of being calm and able to maintain one's position is a must.

The author must *be there* by whatever method - meditation, deep breathing, prayer, centering or whatever. Remember the old show business saying - "The show must go on."

Staying in Character

As previously mentioned, the author must be prepared for anything to happen when in the midst of an interview. Should an overhead light suddenly break free and crash to the floor from the ceiling, the author must be able to maintain his or her composure and not assume that the show will be stopped for a moment or two.

Especially in TV studios, things occasionally get bumped into and fall over. It wouldn't do for the author to get easily rattled.

Sometimes, the best way to handle the situation is to just make light of it. Don't pretend that it didn't happen, as that's not natural.

In 1971 I was producing and hosting a live weekly television variety show. My co-host and I were seated with our guest between us. Directly in front of us was a coffee table on which sat a bouquet of flowers and three coffee cups of water.

I had been casually sitting with my right leg crossed over my left, for the better part of a half hour, when I slowly became aware that my right leg had gone totally numb, the product of long-standing back problem.

Now what to do? I knew if I put my foot down on the floor, I'd have a problem as circulation restored itself. 'Pins and needles' would be very difficult to contain on live TV. Eventually, I just resolved to let the leg be until the interview was over.

A few minutes later, my right hip became numb. This wouldn't do. I shifted my weight slightly and my right leg suddenly went into a spasm, flew off my left knee and cleared the coffee table of flowers and coffee cups.

The guest and I were horrified. This was live TV and there wasn't any going back for retakes. Fortunately, my co-host saved the day. He just smiled, and said, "Neat trick, Larry. What do you do for an encore?" We all broke into laughter, took a short station break to clean up the mess, and the show was saved.

Some people, such as the really great actors, have mastered this to a degree most people would consider impossible.

There's an old film clip of W. C. Fields doing a scene for a movie, when suddenly an earthquake hits. It's instant pandemonium, with lights falling, people running and screaming and walls coming down. Through it all, W. C. never broke character, and told everyone, in his distinctive voice, "Everybody remain calm. It's just a little shaking."

Another story that comes to mind happened at a radio studio in San Francisco, during a live interview.

The host of the show, absently scratching her face during the interview, opened a mole and, unbeknownst to her, blood began to stream down her face. The guest, seeing this and knowing the show was live, just kept on talking as if nothing had happened, casually handed the host his handkerchief and pointed to her face, without saying a word about it.

The host reached her hand up, saw the blood and just about fainted from shock and embarrassment.

The fact that the guest remained calm and carried on *as if nothing had happened* saved the day, even if he did have to cover for her for a few minutes until she regained her composure.

The art of being interviewed is a skill that must be acquired, and there are many 'charm schools' (usually modeling agencies) that exist to assist in this.

The author must be as professional as the host and take the interview just as seriously. That's not to say, *be* serious, just take it seriously and never lose sight of what is riding on the line - his or her success.

Speak With One Voice

It's very important for the author to present the same face and speak with the same voice when doing media interviews and live appearances. Audiences or readers simply don't trust wishy-washy people; they have no credibility. If something happens to change the author's mind over the concept of his or her book, then another book should be written that reflects this new stance.

Don't switch horses in mid-stream.

An Encapsulation of the Art of Being Interviewed

The author should:
- be up for the interview,
- be centered and ready to go,
- dress in a businesslike manner,
- have good timing,
- know and respect studio etiquette,
- dress well,
- remain composed at all times,
- smile into the microphone when speaking,
- think before speaking,
- speak in a relaxed, natural manner,
- speak in everyday terms,
- speak to the audience and not at it,
- use copious examples,
- personalize interview answers,
- speak so that others may experience an encapsulation of the book,

- keep answers short but complete,
- not libel anyone,
- remain calm and objective,
- be patient,
- be consistent,
- present the same face,
- speak with the same voice,
- be prepared to ad-lib,
- and make the experience of the interview a good one for everyone concerned.

The Author As Interview Subject

To be effective as an interview subject, one must be animated, personable and completely professional, for several reasons. An audience will not respond positively to a person who does not come across well on the air. The need is one of being communicative, professional and full of personality and sparkle. Similarly, an interview with someone from the press will not go well if the author is lacking the above qualities.

When doing radio and television interviews, it helps to remember that one is involved in show business. The author must be 'on,' pumped up, and ready to go. This does not mean being half asleep, hung over, or shaking like a leaf. It does mean being enthusiastic and lively.

It's just common sense that a show's guest should arrive ready to do the show, but far too many people show up to be interviewed who have no business being on the air.

To a viewing or listening audience, the author being interviewed *is* the book. Losing sight of this can be disastrous.

If the author does not come across well, his or her message will not be communicated; it will be stopped cold. There is also the very real chance of alienating the audience.

If the author is animated and vibrant, the audience's

attention will be drawn to the interview, as opposed to being turned off by it.

The author *must* feel good, *must* be 'up' for the interview - no less than the host of the show - and *must* be THERE, NOW.

In <u>Way of the Peaceful Warrior</u> Dan Millman talks in depth about this subject. Strange as it may seem, many people go through their daily lives with their minds off somewhere else in a totally different space and time. There's even a slang term for it: 'spaced out.' Spaced out authors just won't cut it on the air.

When the author shows up for an interview, it should mean that he or she is *ready* to be interviewed.

When in front of a microphone or camera, the author must mentally be *there* and *nowhere else* at that time.

Day-dreaming is not conducive to good interviews. Because of that, it's simply not worthwhile for a show host to waste time and energy on someone who does not have the ability to focus on the task at hand! Though the interview might be recorded, there is no guarantee that it will be aired.

> My good friend Avon and I were sitting in a restaurant located in a beautifully restored Victorian house in San Rafael, California. As we relaxed over steaming mugs of herb tea, awaiting our brunch, she told me about the restaurant's philosophy regarding the preparation of its excellent food: Angry people were not allowed in the kitchen or anywhere near food preparation or service.
>
> I was struck by the thought of how incredibly applicable such a rule was to media publicity efforts.

As a general rule, angry authors should stay away from media interviews. For most authors, the main idea is to evoke a *positive* response from the audience, a response that will cause them to seek out the book and not shy away from it.

Of course there are some causes and authors who prefer the angry approach. But for the average author, such emotions just don't come across well on the air.[1]

The most dreaded guests to broadcasters are known in the industry as 'yuppers' or 'nuppers.' Asked a question on the air, such a guest will typically answer in a mono-syllabic fashion, often taking as much as thirty seconds or more to finally answer with a, "Yup," or a "Nup," (Nope). Sometimes these people were very talkative before the show, but just froze up when they realized that the microphones or cameras were on and it was all for real. This presents a real problem for the hapless talk show host.

In the mid-70's, I was producing shows out of a southern California cable television station that offered several public access channels. I already had one public affairs show going, but had an idea about another that I wanted to try.

'Religion Speaks Out' was to have been a non-denominational series, hosted by a local minister, who would interview other ministers on diverse social and community issues.

My existing show had just been selected for consideration for a local Emmy Award nomination. As a result, I was riding high ... the wiz kid who could do no wrong. The station's management quickly cleared the way for a pilot show to be taped.

I set out to find a host and finally settled on a young minister who was quite active in the community.

Next I needed a proper guest.

Much to my surprise, I had trouble finding a minister who was willing to go on camera. I finally found one who reluctantly agreed to come on the show. His reluctance should have served as my first warning, but I was caught up in producing the show and looking forward to making my

---

[1] An excellent resource is the book *Shake the Anger Habit* by Betty Doty and Pat Rooney. Contact The Bookery at 6899 Riata Drive, Redding, CA 96002. (916) 365-8068

directing debut as well.

The day for taping arrived and there sat my reluctant guest, fidgeting in his seat and clearly uncomfortable. My host for the show was all fired up and moving, by comparison, at light speed.

The pilot was a disaster. The guest, upon realizing that the cameras were on and it was all for real, clammed up and would not say anything without considerable prodding from the host.

We finally had to stop and ended up with a five or six minute tape of what was supposed to have been a half hour show.

Needless to say, the pilot was not accepted and I learned an valuable lesson: Do not schedule anyone for an interview who is not both interested in being interviewed *and* personally interesting.

The Need for Charm Schools

Some people are afflicted by microphone fright or are camera shy. Unfortunately, unless it's very obvious, there is just no way to tell beforehand who will react this way and who won't. Some guests may be relaxed and animated before the interview, only to clam up when the interview begins. Frequently, this characteristic can be found in those who did not want to be interviewed, but were talked into it.

If an author has these problems, then he or she should be professionally tutored in the art of being interviewed until the phobia is eliminated. If a positive audience response is desired, there is no other choice in this matter.

There's a lot of work involved in getting a message out to the general public, especially if there is not a huge budget to work with. It doesn't make sense to waste an interview opportunity by turning the audience off.

An interview is only as good as the person being interviewed. As in everything else, there is also an opposite to this. If the *interviewer* is a dud, the interview subject *must* be able to move beyond that problem and *make* the interview good, as he or she is the 'expert' on the subject at hand.

When in doubt about speaking skills, turn to a professional. In just about any major city there are modeling agencies that also train people how to be interviewed and provide a fair amount of actual training on camera and microphone.

Charm schools are not cheap, but are well worth whatever they charge, if they can improve a person's ability to effectively talk on the air.

A Neat Trick

A little trick that can be used to bring about instant relaxation during an interview is for the author to imagine whatever makes him or her happiest as being just behind the person conducting the interview. The author just has to be aware of it and happy that it is there.

The trick is for the author to imagine this without letting his or her imagination run wild. Keep it as simple as possible.

On Being Centered

How many times have we gone into a job interview, spoke before a crowd, or met our prospective in-laws for the first time and felt the total fool? Butterflies begin to flutter inside our tummy and we find ourselves afraid to utter a single word. It's a stressed, spaced-out feeling, and can leave us sort of disjointed and disoriented with everything going on around us. It's an experience common to everyone.

Yet we look at a professional actor or actress, or even a really good salesperson and wonder how they do it. The answer is something called being centered, which could be described as:

an ability to comfortably focus, and when needed, project.

Being centered is a natural condition, probably *the* natural condition.

When we are centered, we project sort of an invisible wall or impenetrable shield around ourselves. When we are not centered, our universe collapses in on us, and anyone or anything can get at us; the least stimuli becomes the straw that will break our back.

Just as a feeling of confidence and well-being goes along with being centered, a feeling of panic and disorientation goes along with the condition of not being centered. We've all felt both conditions.

Life, and especially media work, becomes almost impossible if we are not centered. A good analogy might be the frustration faced when trying to open a combination lock with the wrong combination. The harder we try, the harder it gets. Yet enter the right combination and, magically, the lock opens with just the slightest effort. Such is the feeling of being centered. All our everyday trials and tribulations just seem to blow right past us, mere wisps of energy, almost to be ignored. We suddenly find ourselves the master of all we attempt, and often find ourselves wondering why we were so nervous in the first place. This applies directly to being interviewed.

Under ideal conditions, we would be centered or focused all the time. But the stresses of everyday life, possibly a flat tire on the way to work, a sick child, or a fight with a loved one can throw us off center. These things make it difficult to handle all that is going on around us. This can be disastrous in an interview.

Needless to say, some sort of centering or focusing process must be used by those who plan to do any media work, for one needs to be in control at all times.

While centered: we can easily experience what is going on around us and handle what we must.

While not centered: we become the *effect* of all that is going on around us. This brings about an out of control situation wherein we cannot comfortably experience the events surrounding us, and as a result, corresponding drop in effectiveness occurs.

What has this got to do with getting publicity? In a word, everything. People just can't be effective over the air if they're not centered. Similarly, trying to get bookings while not being centered or focused is a waste of time.

There are many different routes that can be taken to center oneself, such as yoga, meditation and others. Unfortunately, many are time consuming, which makes them impractical for media use.

One of the best centering processes I've come across was developed by my friend Ron Davis, a preeminent researcher in the learning disability field. (Since 1980, Ron's helped thousands of men, women and children gain control of *and eliminate* the adverse effects of their various learning disabilities.)[1]

In developing his really excellent program, part of Ron's research at the Reading Research Council led into the various manifestations of stage fright.

Disorientation, 'choking up,' difficulty with speaking, etc. are stage fright symptoms shared by many people who have a learning disability (only their problem normally comes when confronted with confusion caused by symbols, words, numbers, signs, etc.).

But why were people who didn't have a learning disability sometimes afflicted with many of the symptoms of it while facing a microphone or camera?

Ron Davis has done a lot of media work in his time. In fact, he has both directed television and co-hosted radio

---
[1]The Reading Research Council, 1799 Old Bayshore Highway, Suite #248, Burlingame, CA 94010. (415) 692-8990.

work with this author. Typical of the way that Ron's mind works, once he became interested in the phenomenon of stage fright, he couldn't let it go. What could he do to help someone (like this author) who, despite being a ham behind a microphone or in front of a television camera, dreaded public speaking?

Part of what emerged from that research is the subject of this section, a centering or focusing process that, once learned, is quickly established and works quite well. The technique Ron Davis developed is used here with his permission. It's simple to learn and powerful. Once learned, the process can be done in but a few seconds.

Ron does not refer to the process as 'centering,' but rather calls it "aligning" or "releasing;" but, a rose by any other name ...

The Alignment Process and Releasing

The following was taken from a recording that was done while Ron taught me the process. For the sake of brevity, my responses have been deleted, numbers were added and the tape was edited.

Throughout the process, Ron uses the word 'release' or 'releasing.' *As used for this process, the feeling of release is that relaxed and comfortable feeling that follows a huge sigh.*

After doing the release process, many people could go sound asleep if they didn't open their eyes or think a thought within seconds

By opening our eyes immediately after doing the process we are wide awake right then. As Ron explains it, wide awake and sound asleep are less than an inch apart right at that point in time. So, the thing that can stop us from going to sleep is either opening our eyes or thinking a thought.

(The best time to do this process before a media

appearance would be while sitting in the green room or station lobby.)

Release is more an *absence of something* than a *presence of something*. What we are doing is relaxing the body by creating the *absence of tension*.

As one becomes familiar with the process, it will become almost automatic and very, very fast.

The Alignment Process

For obvious reasons, *do not* do this technique while walking, running, driving or operating machinery!

1. Square up in the chair and get as comfortable as possible.

2. Close your eyes and *feel* your toes down in your shoes.

3. Hold that awareness and locate where your fingers are. Kind of *feel* them from the inside.

4. Expand your awareness from your toes to your ankles and from your fingers to your wrists.

5. Expand from your toes all the way to your knees and from your fingers all the way to your elbows.

6. Expand the feeling all the way up to the hip ... and then all the way up to the shoulders. Be sure to get the inside of your body. Get *all* the insides, all the way up to the neck.

7. Now get all through your neck and all through your head, way up to the skin on the very top of your head. And, don't forget your ears. You want the ears, too. Get it all.

8. Now, flood the *entirety* of it with the feeling of release. Remember that the feeling of release is like a huge sigh. Just let that feeling of release go *flooding* through the system and pour out the ends of your fingers and the ends of your toes. Leave it in a released state.

9. With your awareness only, locate the corners of the room that are above and behind your head.

10. Hold them where they are and locate the corners that are above and in front of your head.

11. Hold them where they are and locate the corners that are below and behind your head.

12. Hold them where they are and locate the corners that are below and in front.

13. Hold them where they are. Now, flood the entire space defined by those eight corners with the feeling of release. Let that feeling of release go beyond your body and completely flood through that space and leave that space in a released state.

14. Fill that space with the essence of who you are. Fill that space and let it feel like you feel when you are you, just being you, at your very best. Let every object and plant and everything in that space have that feeling.

(NOTE: Steps 9 - 14 can also be done by envisioning a sphere surrounding oneself.)

15. Keeping your eyes closed, get the feeling like you are getting up out of the chair and then move around behind the body that is sitting in the chair, and reach down with your imaginary hands and touch the shoulders of the body sitting in the chair.

16. Have the imaginary eyes of the imaginary body that is standing above and behind, open and look down and see the top of the head and the neck and the shoulders of the body sitting in the chair.

17. Hold the corners of the room, and keep the space filled with the essence of you at your best.

18. Get a picture of the imaginary person standing behind you, touching you on the shoulders, while your body is still sitting in the chair. Have the person smile down at you.

19. Open your eyes.

> Other than learning it, my first experience with the above exercise was when I appeared, virtually unprepared, on a television show. I've always enjoyed doing television, but

I've been a little uneasy about the lights and movement just beyond my line of sight. Doing the exercise eliminated the problem.

Similarly, I've since had the odd occasion to speak in public and doing the exercise has virtually eliminated my previous stage fright.

I thought a long time about whether to include the process in this book but then thought, what the heck; it works for me and I've seen it work for others. It is offered here simply as a method that works, maybe not for everybody, but certainly for a great number of the people who try it.

Whatever process one uses, becoming centered, becoming focused, is *vital to doing anything* in media publicity work. Even if one is not afflicted with any form of stage fright, being centered will help considerably with whatever is undertaken.

Quality Control

If several shows have been done and there is little response, it is likely that one of these two things are wrong: either the message being delivered or the person delivering it. Look at each carefully. If the message is okay, then possibly the author needs to be professionally tutored. Of course, there is always the possibility that the general public simply isn't interested in the book. Hopefully, that won't be the case.

Chapter 10

Show Time!

Here's why this book was written: An author is going to sit down in front of a microphone or camera and, whether live or taped, talk about his or her book to a listening or viewing audience. Here's the chance to reach anywhere from a few thousand people to upwards of a million or more. Whether or not anyone responds will depend entirely on what happens in the next few minutes. Every previous chapter in this book has led to this moment and now is when it all begins to come together. The interview will, in large, determine whether the reading, listening or viewing audience buys the author's book. This, is what it is all about.

The publicist should always confirm an interview, by telephone, no later than the day before the scheduled interview.

If the show must be cancelled, it should be done well in advance of the taping time. Rather than just cancel (or worse yet, not show up at all) the publicist should suggest an alternate date. Don't have someone the producer has never heard of show up for the interview.

The author should be completely briefed on the time to be at the station, the proper address, whom to see, etc. Of equal importance is that the author actually shows up on time, ready to be interviewed.

An author should never go alone to do an interview. Someone, preferably the publicist, should tag along. Also, it never hurts for the publicist to meet the station personnel.

Whoever accompanies the author has many roles to fulfill, not the least of which is to see that he or she gets to the station on time, well fed, relaxed, happy and not frazzled by traffic. Since this person should also be the chauffeur, it is important he or she has the directions to the station clearly laid out. If traffic is likely to be a problem, it's important to allow time for that.

Producers prefer to have their guests relaxed and at the station well in advance of the interview. The author should arrive at least 15 minutes early for radio shows, and 45 minutes early for television.

It's vital to differentiate between *taping* time or *on the air* time (for a live show) and *requested arrival* time.

It's always a good idea to allow for extra travel time, just in case. If the destination is only a 20 minute drive, allow at least 30 to 40 minutes. If the drive is to be an hour, then allow an extra 30 to 45 minutes, in addition to at least 15 minutes or so to just take a break. This is very important, because people seldom climb out of a car after a long drive completely relaxed.

The idea is to give the author time to unwind before the interview begins.

The publicist should avoid jammed schedules whenever possible and allow time for breaks in between events. Stop for a decent meal. Sit down and relax. Take the time and it will pay off in the long run with better interviews. If a delay does occur, the publicist should call the station at the earliest possible moment. Just be prepared.

> There's no future in 90 m.p.h. runs down the freeway in the middle of an intense rain storm or something, attempting to get to a station on time. Believe me, I've done it and it's really not worth it. Fun? Sometimes. Exciting? Definitely. Worth the hassle and the risk? No way.

The author must be well informed of what is likely to occur in the interview.

The author should be aware of the 15 or 20 suggested questions that were sent with the initial press kit. However, the author should also be aware that the show host may not necessarily follow the questions.

It's a good idea for the publicist to have several sets of suggested questions and to mix them up between stations. That way the author is always kept on his or her toes and thus avoids sounding repetitious from answering the same questions all the time.

Dressing For The Interview

How should the author and his or her publicist dress? Appearances do count and first impressions are important. Business dress is the order of the day for television and radio. It never hurts to look and act professional - but not stuffy. It's best to dress conservatively, but there is no need to blend into the woodwork.

For television, don't wear white clothing, small pin stripes, or flashy jewelry, as these can sometimes play havoc with the cameras. Men should wear over-the-calf socks.

Studio Etiquette

Studio microphones and cameras should always be considered 'live.' With this in mind, it's a good idea for the author and publicist to make a practice of never saying or doing anything that might embarrass them while on the premises of a station or newspaper. Better safe than sorry.

It's a mistake to arrive at a station with a hoard of people. Two people are fine, maybe three, but don't push it. Broadcast studios are often cramped and extra people just won't fit. Small children, no matter how cute they are, have no place in a station. Needless to say, this *especially* applies to crybabies. Leave them at home.

Some TV stations might ask for additional people if the show is done with a live audience. If this happens, it's not a good idea to issue a blanket invitation to just anyone. Pick audience members with care, especially if there is a chance of them being on the air, however briefly it may be.

Never, ever, interrupt an interview.

Whoever accompanies the author should never interrupt an in-progress interview and this includes off-the-air 'pre-interviews.' It's important that extra people remember not to do anything disruptive such as getting in the way, adding something to the conversation, rustling papers or whatever. That's not to say that the person accompanying the speaker should be robotic - just polite, aware of what is going on and seen but not heard.

In early 1983, I went to Los Angeles for a week-long media blitz with one of my clients. One afternoon we were in Hollywood doing a radio interview in one of the top AM/FM stations in the L.A. basin.

I happened to be sitting in the booth where the interview was being taped, along with my client and the show's host.

About half-way into the one-hour interview, I was shocked to notice that the tape was twisted on the reel-to-reel recorder and realized the interview was not being recorded as a result.

This presented quite a dilemma for me. We were, in the early afternoon, already in our third interview of the day. We were tired and had one or two more to go yet that day. This was an important interview that, with guaranteed re-runs, would net some four hours of air time.

On one hand I was aware of the fact that it was all for naught. On the other hand, I wasn't on my turf, so it wasn't my position to say anything. Had I interrupted the interview there was a very real possibility that I might have disrupted the excellent rapport that existed between my client and the host ... at best. At worst, the host might have resented the interruption and the rapport would have been totally lost.

So, I forced myself to keep my big mouth shut (not an easy thing for me) until the interview was over. At that point, I asked if we might listen to a few minutes of the interview, knowing full well that there would be nothing on the tape.

The host partially rewound the tape and was understandably surprised that nothing was on it. On checking further, he discovered for himself that the tape was twisted just prior to the record head on the recorder. These things happen occasionally, but by his discovering it, as opposed to my pointing it out (and thus making him look amateurish) we were able to have a good laugh.

We took a break and they did the interview a second time. The second interview ended up being even better than the first.

The moral is that by not interrupting and pointing out the host's error, he got to save face and everything turned out all right in the end.

Taking Photographs

Taking pictures of the interview usually doesn't present a problem, as long as the station personnel are informed of it beforehand. They will indicate when pictures can be taken.

When taking pictures on a TV set, high-speed film is preferable because a flash isn't necessary. In radio stations, a flash wouldn't be a problem, but it could interrupt the interview. Pictures are thus best taken before or after the interview.

Meeting Other Guests

Perhaps we should take a little time to talk about celebrities, athletes, politicians and other guests.

People who are in the entertainment business, sports or politics often appear larger than life to the general public. As a result, some people don't know how to act around them.

Many stations, especially TV stations, will have so-called 'green rooms' for the guests (and their entourage) to relax in before their interview segment.

It's not uncommon to bump into a well-known actor or actress, singer, politician or athlete who is also waiting to go on the air.

Often, the producer or production assistant will introduce everyone, but not always.

On meeting a celebrity or politician, just be cool and professional. This person, even though a public figure, is just another person. Often hounded by their public, celebrities, athletes and politicians tend to feel safe within the confines of a station and this should be respected; they may live a public life but they do have a right to moments of peace and quiet.

Basically, most celebrities are just normal - if incredibly talented - people. Some celebrities - and most politicians - have egos bigger than a mountain. Yet others are terribly shy and insecure. Voicing an admiration of their work or achievements probably won't bother most celebrities, but don't push it by asking for autographs and such. If celebrities wish to pursue a conversation, fine. Otherwise, let them be.

The green room is viewed and treated as neutral turf for all concerned. It's not necessary to talk to the people there. But, by all means, don't hassle them: leave them alone.

The Tactile Thrills

Never touch *anything* at a station (other than to adjust a microphone - more on this later). This sounds really basic, but many people are fascinated by blinking lights and needles moving on a meter. Patch cords also seem to be particularly fascinating, as do feeds from a news-wire machine.

Many people seem to exhibit sort of a tactile sense starvation upon arriving at a station and need to touch and feel everything. This is, no doubt, an unconscious effort to center themselves, make themselves more familiar with unfamiliar territory, but it's important to resist the urge.

Some producers will offer their guests a nickel tour of the station so that the guest feels more at home. Some producers will also want to go over a few points they'd like to touch on in the interview, but this is not necessarily the way others operate. The guest might walk through the door, be ushered directly into the studio and suddenly the interview is underway.

My first director at KFRC was a very talented lady who had a most interesting interview technique in that her pre-interview *was* the interview. She would sit the guest down in the studio and casually begin chatting, as if to gather information and to get to know each other before the actual interview began.

Unknown to the guest, the microphones were 'live' and the tape was rolling. This would go on for 15 or 20 minutes, at which point she would thank the very surprised guest and direct the person out the door. The tape would later be edited into a finished show. This is a very effective technique and results in even the most terrified guest being relaxed.

Taping the Interview

It's a mistake to automatically assume the station will give out a tape or 'dub' of the interview. Tapes, especially video tapes, are expensive. If stations automatically gave out tapes of each and every person they interviewed ... well, it's easy to see how this could get expensive for them.

For a 30 minute radio interview, take a 'C60' cassette tape (30 minutes per side), 'C90' for a 45 minute show, and 'C120' for a one hour interview. Any good, low noise tape will do the job. The station might want to mail it out later, especially if the show is to be edited. As a rule, the stations are pretty good about doing this.

Television is something altogether different. One drawback of having a videotape done at the station is that it may not be compatible with home equipment, so it's better to have someone tape the interview at home on a VCR. Don't take a VHS or camcorder-formatted tape to have the station record the show as the they might not be able to use it.

Ask at the time of the interview scheduling what type of tape is required. It's not uncommon for a TV station to charge a minimal fee (usually around $25 to $50) for duplicating a supplied tape. But, again, television station equipment may not be compatible with home equipment. This is not a hard and fast rule, however. It's best to ask up front.

Critiquing his or her interviews can be an invaluable exercise for an author, especially because one will often see or hear things that went right past while in the middle of the interview. This is especially true of television interviews, where the guest can be seen fidgeting, sitting off-center, or leaning to one side (a real problem with me).

I once had a client who had a very distracting habit of pulling at his moustache and rubbing his nose as he spoke. Although several people had mentioned it to him, it didn't become real to him until he saw it for himself on TV. The next interview, his hands remained firmly planted in his lap and everything went well.

Remember that stations own the copyrights to any shows that they produce. Tapes of their shows cannot legally be duplicated for distribution or sale without written permission from each particular station involved. This applies whether a tape was received from a station or it was taped with privately owned equipment directly off the air.

To be legal, copyrighted material must be acknowledged. In most cases, something like, "(Segment) videotape courtesy of (station call letters), (city and state)" will suffice. At any rate, stations are familiar with the rules, so check with them before using their tapes for air play elsewhere.

If pre-recorded tape or slides are provided to a station for inclusion in an interview, the station must be informed if they are from another station.

If a privately produced tape is provided to a station, then whoever produced the tape owns the copyright and not them; but be aware of the copyright legalities involved.

Giving a station one's own tape, pictures or slides for them to use *automatically releases the copyright for that use*. If the station reruns the segment, they do not have to gain permission from the copyright holder to use it again.

Keeping the Mouth and Throat Moist

Dry mouths can really be a problem when on the air, so when being interviewed on radio or TV, it's important to keep one's mouth moist. Similarly, dry, hacking coughs are extremely distracting. Some radio stations will permit coffee, tea water or soft drinks in the broadcast booth, but don't count on it.

Cough drops work quite well for keeping the mouth moist, but it's important to not let them get in the way of talking.

I was coming down with a cold and arrived at the studios with a handful of cough drops. My engineer got on my case about the noise the wrappers made as I unwrapped them. Fortunately, he clued me in before we went on the air.

Microphones are quite sensitive and the sound of a cough drop being unwrapped comes across quite clearly and is very distracting. Similarly, the sound of a cough drop clicking against one's teeth will most likely be picked up.

If there is a possibility a cough drop might be needed during the interview, my engineer's advice was to unwrap it beforehand and leave it sitting on the table, where it can be silently picked up.

Cough drops are especially important when one has a sore throat or is getting over or coming on to a cold.

Avoid cough drops or cough preparations that contain any sort of anesthetic as the vocal cords can become numb and then a very real problem presents itself.

Throat sprays can be used in the place of a cough drop. One trick is to dissolve a cough drop in the mouth and drink a cup of water just prior to air time.

Chewing gum will also keep the mouth moist but, here again, there is the danger of it popping or the sound of chewing coming through the mike, so leave it behind.

Some radio studios will have a button in front of the guest marked 'cough.' This button will temporarily cut off the microphone if it is held down, to allow the guest to cough, should the need arise. (Remember to release the button!)

Dealing With Intestinal Troubles

Gas, heartburn or indigestion problems can be extremely distracting when on the air. Tummy rumbles, if they can be heard by the ear, can be picked up by microphones.

If one is disposed towards intestinal problems, then preparations to eliminate them must be taken ahead of time, before sitting down at the microphone or going on camera.

Several over-the-counter drugs exist that help to dissolve intestinal gas. Of course, one must follow the directions on the label or, if necessary, see a doctor for prescription medicine.

What to Expect ...

When dealing with the media, as with life, expect the unexpected.

... Radio

Allowing for a few differences, most radio shows will be similar.

The guest and his or her entourage arrive at the station and check in with the receptionist, who needs to know just who they are and who they need to see (unless instructed otherwise, this will be the producer or show host). They'll be asked to have a seat in the lobby or perhaps ushered into the station's green room. Often, coffee and tea will be available. They may or may not be offered a tour of the station.

The main idea is to get familiar with the station and relax. With but a few exceptions, the station personnel are going to do whatever they can to make their guests comfortable.

Normally, about five or six minutes before the interview begins, the guest(s) will be ushered into the studio and seated before a microphone. Whoever accompanied the guest will probably be able to monitor the interview from the engineer's booth, but not always. Depending on the show host and station rules, extra people may be allowed into the studio. If desired, it's at this point that the show host or engineer should be given a cassette tape to record.

The author should reach out and adjust the microphone so that it is about four to five inches from his or her mouth. On the air, the author should not speak directly into a microphone, but rather *across* the front of it, diagonally. Adjusting the microphone does two things: First, it makes it easier for the engineer to balance the sound levels, and second, it makes the author a little more familiar with his or her surroundings.

The show's host may or may not go over a set of questions and may just sit and chat for awhile. This is to break the ice and get a comfortable rapport going with the guest. Many producers and hosts like to meet the guest in the green room or lobby and chat for a few minutes over a cup of coffee before going into the studio. This is calculated to calm the guest down and, as mentioned above, develop a rapport.

About two minutes before the show is to start, the engineer will usually ask for sound levels (have the guest and show host talk for a few seconds to adjust the microphones) and may ask the guest to move the microphone one way or another, lean into it, or whatever. (Note: Not all radio shows are done with a show host and engineer. Sometimes the engineering is done by the show host.)

Usually, the show's host (or hosts) will wear headphones. It's not necessary for the guest to wear them.

Sometimes the headphones will be connected to the engineer's booth so that the engineer or producer can offer suggestions to the host while the interview is in progress. This is especially true in TV, where the hosts are seen wearing clear plastic devices that look like tiny hearing aids. The show's producer will often sit in the engineering booth with a bio of the show's guest and prompt the show's host from it. Sometimes material countering what the author is talking about will be brought forth.

Some guests get nervous and start squirming around in the chair, leaning back, or rocking the chair from side to side. This will quickly put a guest on the engineer's hit list as it screws up the delicate balance job he or she has done on the microphone sound levels. Leaning too close to the microphone will cause sound distortion; popping 'Ps' and hissing 'Ss.' Squirming from side to side or leaning backwards, pulling away from the microphone, will cause the person to sound as if he or she is talking from across the room.

When the engineer calls for sound checks, the author should

just assume a comfortable position, adjust the microphone accordingly and speak from that position the entire show. The author should remember not to tap fingers or toy with a pen or pencil on the table (this often comes across the mikes as a booming sound). Tapping feet can also cause problems.

It should be noted that not all microphones will be stood or hung on adjustable stalks in front of the guest. Some of them (especially for TV) clip onto a shirt or tie. Some others lay on the table and look just like a flat piece of metal with a wire sticking out of it.

Just before the show starts, whether live or taped, the engineer, director or show host will call out, "Stand by." This is normally a 10-second time cue. The author should just sit quietly and take his or her cues from the host.

When talking on the air, it's important for the author to speak normally and smile into the microphone. The best interviews are done in this manner. Even interviews about very serious subjects come across better if everyone is smiling. That doesn't mean being flip or cute; just pleasant.

Quite often, the show's host will be seen to anxiously look towards the engineer's booth or hold up hastily scribbled notes towards the engineer's window. While this is distracting, the author should just ignore it and continue as if the interview were nothing more than a conversation with a friend, although it admittedly takes some concentration to pull it off.

If the host is working without an engineer, he or she might be setting up cart machines, reading other copy, adjusting microphone sound levels, etc., which can be very distracting. The host might even ask a question, stand up, take the headphones off and leave the room while the guest is answering it! Sounds nuts, but it's been known to happen. (No one ever claimed radio people were sane!)

Regardless, the guest should just continue on as if nothing untoward was happening. Remember that, unless things really get out of hand, the listening audience is aware of *none* of this ... they only know what they hear. Such is the magic of radio.

It was 6:00 a.m. on a Sunday morning. Ron Davis and I were sitting in the broadcast booth for a live interview at the old KYUU-FM in San Francisco.

It was obvious that the show's host was having problems with the interview. From the way he was acting, it was most likely due to some outside problem; maybe he had had a fight with his wife or something. Whatever, he was getting far too serious for an early-morning Sunday show.

Suddenly I saw him smile and suppress a giggle. Looking around, I saw that the engineer (the engineer's booth was behind Ron and I) had taken a paper toilet seat cover and draped it around his head. The paper flap covered his face ... on it were written the words, "LIGHTEN UP!"

The show host relaxed and the rest of the interview went fine.

As mentioned earlier, the author should keep his or her answers brief and to the point, but also ensure that plenty of detail is given. It's a mistake to ramble off on long, technical or esoteric explanations as the audience will quickly be lost. Of course, should the show host ask for such an explanation, that is a different story. But, even then, the less said the better. (Keep It Simple, Stupid.)

The author should mention the title of his or her book three or four times during the course of the interview. Mention also where the book can be purchased locally. If it is not available on local shelves, mention the address where it can be ordered.

There's nothing sacred about recording tape. If the show is being taped and a mistake is made, the engineer can always stop the tape, edit out the mistake and then restart. But, unless the mistake is a particularly gross one, the author shouldn't ask for this to happen.

The best interviews flow smoothly with no breaks. If a mistake is made, it's best to make light of it and then go on; this actually makes the guest sound more human.

If the interview is being done live, it may be broken up by commercials, public service announcements or whatever. It's best to just go with the flow.

Authors have a certain mystique about them and will generally be treated by station personnel as if they had been interviewed hundreds of times before. Even if he or she has never been interviewed previously, the author should just take the ball and run with it as a professional.

The author shouldn't attempt to hog the microphone or assume a superior position to the show host. Also, the author shouldn't attempt to 'talk down' to the audience.

When the interview is over, the guest is usually just thanked and ushered out the door. If the show was being done live, there may not be much of a chance to chat afterwards, but the author and publicist should remember to thank the host. After the interview, the publicist can retrieve the copy of the show if a tape was left with the engineer beforehand.

A word about etiquette. Changes sometimes occur quickly in the broadcast world. Today's beginning intern could very well be tomorrow's producer or show host.

Politeness and good manners are the keys to future dealings with all station or media personnel.

... Television

Generally speaking, television isn't that much different from radio, except that the sense of sight has been added to that of sound. With television, it's very important to look and dress well. Appearances count and the wise guest is dressed in a business-like manner.

Upon arriving and checking in, the guests and their

entourage will either wait in the lobby or be escorted to the green room. A television station's green room is normally presided over by the show's producer, a production assistant or an intern. Among other duties, it is their responsibility to usher the guests to the set in time for their segment, and then usher them back to the green room or to the reception area when their segment is over. Whoever is overseeing the green room will also issue any necessary instructions to the guests. A television is usually set up for the guests to watch the show in-progress.

The author may be ushered off for make-up. (If the guest has any skin allergies, its best to inform the make-up person. However, most all make-up used on television is hypo-allergenic.)

Back in the green room, the author will usually have anywhere from 15 to 45 minutes to simply sit and relax. As mentioned earlier, there may or may not be celebrities or political figures present. When talking to anyone in the green room, don't attempt to sell them on anything; they've got their own topic and are likewise authorities in their own respective fields. For a live TV show, someone will usually brief the author on what the host(s) intend to cover in the interview.

Very seldom is the guest immediately ushered onto the set, but this can happen, so it's best to be prepared for it.

Whether shot in a studio or on a sound stage set, a television show, done live or taped, can be confusing to the uninitiated. There can be three or four cameras, movable overhead lights, and dozens of people watching and working on the show, or even an entire audience. One is quick to notice a lot of movement behind the cameras and off to the side.

Especially noticeable are the floor director and the studio's TV monitor. Despite the temptation to watch them, the author should ignore both. It's always apparent when someone is watching the floor director. Likewise, it's always apparent when a guest would rather watch his or her image on the monitor than participate in the interview. Eye movements are *especially* noticeable under the bright lights.

Even though the show may be shot in an area the size of a couple of basketball courts, the author should develop the capacity to think of the set as being a closed studio. The author should learn to ignore the lights, cameras and the action and just talk to the host(s). The trick is to ignore everything else, create a little world where nothing else matters or is happening outside of the immediate set and get into the interview. The author should talk to the host of the show and not to the cameras.

Of course, this all changes when there is a live audience and audience participation. The feeling that one is under a microscope is inescapable. There's no getting around it … the author is on display and will sink or swim within the confines of the interview.

When doing a television show, it's best to assume that one is always on camera. In reality, that's what is happening, but the technical director will switch 'takes' between cameras constantly throughout the show. Of course, stations normally only use the picture from only one camera at a time. With this in mind, it's important to never do anything embarrassing on the set. No matter how urgent the need to scratch whatever itch makes itself known (and they always will make themselves known) the author should just learn to ignore them!

I once participated in a three-person interview at a rather low-budget TV station in Chicago during a hot and humid August afternoon. The studio's air conditioning unit had gone out and, under the lights, the temperature quickly soared past the 100-degree mark. Now, I am not a small man, and bodies like mine tend to melt profusely when the temperature and humidity are high.

Out of a half-hour segment, the director was forced to pull the camera off me five or six times, and zoom in on the host or the other guest, at which point an intern would quickly scamper in and dry my face and neck with a towel.

It didn't occur to me until sometime later that it must have appeared odd, showing me drowning in perspiration in one shot, dry in the next and then drowning again in the next.

It's important that the author have the ability to follow directions and move quickly, especially if the show is live.

The guest on the first segment of a television a show sometimes has the luxury of taking some time to get adjusted to the set and the lights and settled into the seat before the interview starts. Guests who have following segments are ushered in between commercials and quickly seated. They are wired for sound and sometimes have barely fifteen or twenty seconds to adjust before the interview is underway again. It's entirely possible that the guest might not have any time at all to develop any sort of rapport with the host or hostess. Television is known to move, by comparison with radio, very quickly.

The proper attitude is for the author to be mentally ready for the interview from the instant he or she steps into the station lobby; ready for a camera and lights to replace the receptionist and the interview to be under way. Equally important is for the author to allow the station personnel to be totally in control. They will indicate when to move to the set and when to get up and leave it.

The publicist should also remember to bring along a fresh change of clothes for the author. If the author's hair tends to get windblown, a small hair dryer is a must. Ever wonder how guests on shows that are taped during stormy weather always look neat and unrumpled? That's how they do it; fresh clothing, hair dryers and sometimes hair spray and make-up. It's important that the author look professional, cool and calm.

... The Press

Press interviews can take place just about anywhere. Whether in the home office, out in the field or in the publication's office, they seem to fall into a predictable pattern. In the old days, newspapers used to run news crews like television; a reporter and photographer. These days it's not uncommon for the reporter to carry a 35 mm camera and record the interview either on a cassette tape or simply take notes, although a crew might still be used.

Press interviews are quite different from public affairs or entertainment radio or TV interviews, in that the press people are, as a group, highly cynical. Regardless of what is said, and this applies to electronic media news people as well, or how well it's said, reporters (but not necessarily book review editors) will almost always seek out other opinions or dig for something negative. The trick is to be especially careful about what one is saying when around the press. Unlike radio and television, a press reporter may be friendly during the interview and then write a totally negative review. Normally, with radio or television what you see is what you get (although a piece will often be edited to reflect a negative slant).

The author should remember as well to mention the title of the book, but with the press, don't belabor it by repetition. Once the title is printed in the article, it's there and not likely to go away. Mention also where the book can be obtained.

A vital point to remember is that most radio and TV interviews will be on either public affairs or entertainment shows (including the 'morning magazine' formats), whereas interviews with the print media almost always mean dealing with reporters or book review editors.

On Patience

It has been said that the best laid plans of mice and men often go astray. This applies to the radio and television business as well. Equipment breaks and delays occur. When at a station, or at a newspaper office for an interview, the author should be patient as a rock if something goes wrong. Rest secure in the knowledge that the proper personnel are doing whatever they can to get things rolling again. If delayed to the point where later appointments are threatened, the publicist should call ahead with this information. People at the stations will usually work with their guests with this. This is where carrying the media cards or the day's itinerary sheet comes in handy, especially when operating away from home base.

A Disturbing Trend

There is a trend in broadcasting today to upset the audience - "Stir up the rabble" - and I find this most disturbing. However, like it or not, such programming is a fact of life and something we must live with. Of course, not all stations or interview shows are interested in doing this, but we must be aware that *some* are and be prepared for them. The rabble-rousing interview shows will generally be found airing in the late-afternoon and in the evening, before midnight. How they are handled is purely personal.

Chapter 11
After The Interview

Common courtesy dictates that the producer and host of a show be thanked for the interview, but it's surprising at just how often this is forgotten. Sometimes, especially after TV shows, the guests are ushered off the set following their segment and may not get the chance to thank the appropriate people face to face. If that occurs, the author should mail a 'thank you' card as soon as possible.

I keep stressing this point throughout this book: it never hurts to maintain good relations with everyone in the media. This is a must for any author to successfully promote his or her book! The author and publicist would be well-advised to remember that today's beginning intern could very well be tomorrow's hot shot producer or show host.

Everyone deserves a pat on the back for a job well done. If the interview went particularly well, send a letter of commendation to the station's manager regarding the producer and the show host. It never hurts to plant seeds of kindness as they can grow to surprising fullness in time.

Sally Hall was my co-host and sometimes producer for several years but before that, she was just a 'gofer' for my show. Typically she would greet the guests, fetch coffee and such. Many guests totally ignored Sally but I always asked about her perceptions of the individual guests and valued her judgement. Her perception of each individual guest weighed heavily when it came to possibly ask a guest to return for another interview. Sally is quite a few years younger than myself, and thus saw the guests in a totally different light. Her advice was so sound that I finally made her co-host of my show.

To not be sexist, I must say, that as a man, I'm a believer in the intuition of a woman.

Whenever possible, it's a good idea to listen to, or view, tapes of completed interviews a few days after they have been done.

Waiting a few days before reviewing tapes allows them to be experienced in a more objective light and then notes can be taken to allow for improvements on up-coming interviews. In the light of a new day, it's amazing to hear things which went on during the interview that, at the time, were missed. By reviewing the tapes, it's possible to continually fine-tune the author's performance.

When doing a number of interviews on the same book, there is a natural tendency to deviate some from the original concept. This can cause problems as there is a need to be consistent.

By the same token, reviewing completed interviews will allow the delivery style to be adjusted to the point where it communicates best.

Authors should avoid the trap of doing shows by rote (this is where prepared questions can be a real hazard, as the tendency is to answer them the same each time).

Each interview must be fresh, even if two or more interviews are being done daily.

After the interview airs and there is some idea of the response, it never hurts to send another letter to the producer with this information - especially if the response was particularly good. This has a dual purpose, as it helps the producer to know something of the response and, as mentioned earlier, it plants a little seed in the producer's head that the audience really responded to the author's interview. This comes in handy for publicizing one's *next* book!

It's not a good idea to try to PR the producers with phony tales of fantastic response; they pretty much know what their audience is and can spot anyone trying to pull something over on them.

A letter from the author saying he or she was quite pleased with the response carries tremendous weight by itself. With that in mind, the station might like to have the author back again (although don't mention it at this time).

If the interview went particularly well, the station may even re-run it at a later date.

Stations will also receive inquiries about shows they air, but their guests usually won't know about these.

An author's relationship with a particular show's producer begins with the initial contact; it is up to the publicist and author to develop it from that point on. This is especially important for self-published authors who might like to return for an additional interview sometime down the road. Make as many friends in the media as possible, as this can pay off with both re-runs and additional bookings down the road.

Media people are in the communications' business; communication is their stock in trade. Stay in communication with them, pat them on the back when they do a good job and be available to them whenever they desire an interview or even just background information.

Do this, and it will really pay off in the long run.

During the years that I was the publicist for Ron Davis' learning disability program, we became friends with numerous people in the broadcast industry. One of our new friends was the producer/host of a weekly half hour show over a small FM station. She eventually left that station and now does the same thing over 30 different stations across the country, via satellite.

Our friendship remains to this day. Ron has appeared twice on her network and has had numerous reruns as well.

This is a perfect example of what can be accomplished by

making friends with people at the various stations.

Also, when I became the general manager of a radio station, I frequently ran previous interviews I had done with Ron.

The point is, if a show's producer *likes* the person being interviewed, one interview can result in additional ones. Conversely, if the producer is turned off by a certain interview guest, he or she just might stop further interviews with the offending guest.

Chapter 12

The Publicity Tour

Sooner or later, the author will want to take the show on the road to other stations outside the immediate area, a publicity tour. A publicity tour here is defined as being any trip that takes all day or necessitates staying overnight. This can be across the state or across the country. Often such trips will include many media appearances and press interviews, with possibly a personal appearance or two thrown in as well.

Complete planning is the key to successful road trips. Not only will the lack of proper and thorough preparation lead to the aforementioned frantic speed runs down freeways, there is also the added confusion (and maybe even danger) of being on unfamiliar roads. Traffic in major cities is bad enough, but trying to find a location in a strange city can leave a driver with his hands full in a hurry. Factor in some inclement weather and the fact that one can become easily disoriented in an unfamiliar city and the problems and potential danger become very apparent.

It's far better to arrive early and have to sit in a green room for awhile than it is to fight traffic and arrive frazzled just minutes before air time.

The itinerary for a publicity tour should be set *at least* a month in advance of the scheduled departure date. The itinerary may have to be adjusted before or after the departure date.

The author should not take off on a publicity tour alone. A second person, preferably the publicist, should be along to handle the details.

Plans that leave nothing to chance, including budgeting, need to be completed well in advance of the trip. These plans must then be followed *to the letter* as much as possible. Sometimes things can and do happen to screw up the best laid plans, and this often necessitates a complete change in the itinerary.

Up to date highway and street maps should be obtained at least two or three weeks in advance and locations plotted on them. (I highly recommend the American Automobile Association maps.) Become familiar with the directions laid out on the media cards by studying the map.

Especially important is the ability to orient oneself in a strange city by finding easily identifiable locations or landmarks and plotting them on the maps. It helps to orient the day around a certain location, such as the hotel, and then go in sequence from one event to another.

Along with knowing the location for a given time, one must also know how to get to the next location. What will traffic be like? What will be the travel time between locations? Is there any ongoing road construction? These things need to be known.

If the plan calls for taking taxis around the city, then information must be on hand as to their availability and estimated travel time between locations. Each station can usually give information on the general picture beforehand.

Some people are natural pathfinders, yet others couldn't find their way out of a closet. Because of this there is the need for complete planning and the need to have an up-to-date picture of what is happening in the scheduled city, *especially regarding road work or closures and traffic patterns.* In our own back yards we tend to take so much for granted, and often do not think of what it would be like to be a stranger on the scene. Plan to leave nothing to chance, and remember that if an opening is left for something to go wrong, it most likely will.

Even with complete planning, something can always go wrong.

Thorough planning allows for minimal effort and the full utilization of available time.

As mentioned above, the itinerary for a publicity tour should be set at least a month in advance of the departure date. This means that the stations must be contacted at least *ten to twelve weeks* in advance.

With travel costing what it does, it just makes sense to get the most out of the trip. When going to another city, even for just one day, it's best to do multiple interviews, if possible.

When initially contacting the media within a particular city, the publicist should concentrate first on the news-talk radio stations and TV stations with morning or afternoon interview shows. (How to find out? Call in advance and ask the station to send a program schedule.) Second would be newspapers and other radio and TV stations.

The actual scheduling is often somewhat tricky. The idea is to concentrate on the major media first without ignoring the secondary media sources.

The publicist should just play it by ear. This is the reason for contacting the major media sources as much as ten to twelve weeks in advance, so that they can be scheduled first. (A yearly day-by-day wall calendar is a must for this sort of operation.) The publicist should be sure to mention that a publicity tour is being planned and list the dates for the 'window of opportunity.'

For a tour that ranges from Atlanta to Los Angeles or even just a few hundred miles away, enough appearances must be lined up to make the trip worthwhile. (However, it should be noted that, once committed to a publicity tour, it's best to stick to whatever interview bookings were lined up, no matter how many or how few they happen to be.)

When scheduling an interview, speaking appearance or book signing, allow time for the next interview, *even if it has not yet been set*. Allow at least 45 minutes to an hour from the end of one event to the beginning of the next. Keep in mind that the time at a station will be at least 45 minutes for a half hour show, and as long as an hour and a half for an hour long show.

Away from home base, time tends to do some weird things. With this in mind, the publicist should learn to build time 'pads' into the schedule. For a 30 minute radio interview that begins at 2:00 p.m., plan to be there at 1:45 p.m. and figure to be there until at least 2:45 p.m. - a 15 minute time pad on each side of the interview.

These 'time pads' are necessary because anything can happen, from an equipment failure, to the station's previous interview being overly long. The author doesn't need to be sitting in the middle of an interview and worried about getting to the next one on time. Time pads are especially true for television. A given segment might be five to six minutes of an hour-long show, yet the station will want the guest to be there up to 45 minutes early for make-up and possibly a pre-interview.

In most cases, the particular television show segment that a guest might have cannot be predicted when scheduling. Even though a guest might only have a short segment of the show, the station's producer will want the guest there for its entire length.

For a half-hour television show that has a requested arrival time of 12:45, plan on an actual arrival time of 12:15 - 12:30. This would normally put the show starting at 1:30. Plan on being at the station until 1:45 or 2:00 unless informed otherwise.

The above paragraph is one more very good reason for having more than one person on a road trip. Should the schedule get jumbled and begin to fall apart, the author can go on the air, relaxed and confident that his or her backup (preferably the publicist) will make whatever calls are necessary and straighten the schedule out. This is a primary reason for building generous time pads into the daily schedule ... also, it's not a good idea to have the author's day jammed with interviews. It's far better to space the interviews out.

When flying from one location to another, the possibility of jet-lag must also be considered and planned for accordingly. If going across country, it's best to arrive a day early.

In actual practice, quite a bit of time will be spent waiting in green rooms or station lobbies. But it's best to not plan on this. Just use the time pads properly and then follow the day as it develops. It's far better to be early and have to cool your heals for awhile than to wander in late with a tale of woe.

No producer wants to see a guest stressed out from an overly burdensome schedule. Don't attempt to set up more than two appointments for each morning and no more than three (half-hour interviews) in the afternoon, with possibly another one in the evening. Five to six interviews in one day can take a lot out of anyone.

It's better to work with the stations rather than fight a schedule that gets screwed up. If there's a possibility of being late for the next interview, the publicist should call the following station and inform the producer what is happening. It might not be a problem, or the producer might want to reschedule.

Producers are used to working with people on publicity tours and will generally be a little flexible, but the publicist shouldn't depend on it. Just work with them, stay in communication and everything should work out.

Sometimes, it might be necessary to extend a trip an extra day or two for rescheduling of shows … in fact, plans for the tour should include budgeting for just this event.

As mentioned before, it's very important to include time in the schedule for an occasional break in the action; stop and smell the roses; have a relaxing meal (forget about gobbling down fast food). Avoid heavy gas- or indigestion-producing foods. Small, light meals are best when on the road. Some people have intestinal problems when traveling, probably from water differences or food preparation.

The publicist should carry a supply of anti-gas, heartburn and diarrhea medicine from interview to interview if these things are likely to be a problem. Activated charcoal (available in capsules at health food and drug stores) is also good for handling diarrhea. A good supply of aspirin or other painkillers should also be on hand, along with any prescription medications. The author should avoid cold or cough preparations that cause drowsiness. The aforementioned spirulina tablets can help keep the author and publicist energized, alert, awake and better able to handle the stresses of the road.

When doing several interviews or personal appearances in one day, the author *must* develop the capacity to leave the last interview behind and approach the next in a totally new unit of time and frame of mind.

Similarly, the author *must* approach each interview as the most important interview ever!

It must be understood that, to the audience, the interview the author is in at that particular moment is likely the first interview of *that day*.

It's not uncommon to come off of a boring interview only to find that the next host is a real dynamo. This is why there is a need to just stop occasionally, have a cup of coffee or a bite to eat and then start all over again. Each interview needs to be approached as a separate entity; the author must approach each interview, relaxed and confident, as if it were the only one that day.

Occasionally, a jammed schedule cannot be avoided and when that happens it will just have to be handled as best as possible. The publicist should plan for the ideal scene, but be prepared for anything.

Once the schedule for the publicity tour is set, the next step is to set up hotel or motel, flight, and rent-a-car reservations as necessary. (It's a good idea to check with the local Chamber of Commerce or Convention Bureau when first beginning to plan, because trying to find a place to stay and do a major media blitz could be a problem if several conventions were scheduled for the chosen city at the same time.)

Do not make the mistake of simply arriving in a particular city and then seeking somewhere to stay. It's just not worth the trouble.

Again, remember to distinguish between *city of origin* (location of broadcast studios) and *city of license* (where the station is licensed to) designations.

It may seem out of sequence to set the schedule before the accommodations, but it's that way for a very good reason. After the itinerary is set, look the maps over closely. Plan to stay as much in the center of the bookings as is possible, thus shortening travel time and allowing a centrally-located base from which to operate. One of the primary reasons for this, other than the obvious convenience, is that accidents can, and sometimes do, happen; clothing can get soiled and torn. Being centrally located will ease things considerably if something like this happens.

When working a full-day's schedule it's a good idea for the author to plan on changing into a fresh set of clothes once or twice throughout the day - especially if the interviews are being conducted in hot, humid cities or on TV.

Once the itinerary is set, the publicist should get directions from the hotel or motel to the first scheduled appearance. Next, contact each of the other stations, in sequence, and get directions to the next scheduled appointment (i.e. ask at the first station how to get to the second station; ask the second station how to get to the third, and so on). The publicist should do this for each day, beginning with directions to the first appointment of the day.

It's important to inquire about any known road work or any other factors that could lead to delays. The publicist should get the big picture and mark important road information on the maps. Especially important is what roads to avoid at certain times of the day due to heavy traffic.

The directions must be explicit and simple. The publicist should put them on the back of the media cards in pencil (so they can be changed) and number each card on the front in sequence and by date.

All of the interview locations should be listed on a master itinerary, with a duplicate made up for someone at home base to follow, as there is always the possibility that a station that earlier turned the author down has had second thoughts, now wants an interview and might call home base. Someone at home base needs to know where the author and publicist can be reached at all times. Either have the home base leave messages at the hotel or call the next scheduled stations, per the itinerary sheet, and leave a message.

The itinerary and maps must be reviewed at the beginning of each day and as the day progresses.

The publicist should keep the itinerary on a clipboard or in a folder, and cross off each scheduled appearance as it is done and move on to the next. Take the next card in sequence and follow the directions to the next location.

As mentioned earlier, it's best to go to the location and then take a break as opposed to taking a break first and then rushing around to try and find the next appointment. Get there first and then relax.

There is always the temptation to jam an interview in between two other interviews that are, say, an hour apart. Since most interviews will average around twenty minutes, this looks easy. In actual practice, however, it just doesn't work.

Whoever accompanies the author on a publicity tour should also be the driver and navigator, there to keep the author cheered up as well as ensuring that everything goes right. The second person must be very well organized and not someone who thrives on cutting time short and arriving at the last moment. This person must do anything, including lying about the necessary arrival time on the itinerary, if the author is a habitually late person. This is an important job and should not be taken lightly. Hundreds or thousands of miles away from home, there are pressures which simply don't exist in one's own back yard. Again, it bears keeping in mind that time often becomes distorted when away from home base.

When going out of town, even if traveling just a hundred miles or so, it's best to arrive the night before a morning interview. Get some rest and arrive for the interview looking fresh and composed; not burned out from getting up before dawn and driving two or three hours or, as mentioned earlier, suffering the effects of jet-lag.

Remember always that television is a visual medium and that radio is an audio medium. Someone looking rumpled or sounding tired or ill on television will not come across well. Someone sounding tired and wasted on radio will not come across well. Either situation may be a waste of valuable media exposure.

What it boils down to is this: When going to go to all the trouble of setting up and doing a publicity tour out of town, do it right and get as much out of it as possible. Make the best use of time. Haphazard planning has no place here.

Some final notes about publicity tours: Despite gearing up for the trip several months in advance, keep the local bookings going as well. The publicist should not become myopic and focus only on the immediate tour.

The publicist should set up local interviews for after the tour. These must be scheduled in advance of leaving. It's important for the author and publicist to develop the ability to live and think, bookings wise, at least two months in advance. This is where the yearly (or at least a quarterly) wall-mounted daily planning calendar comes into its own. It helps to be able to look at it, and with a mere glance, see what days are scheduled several months in advance.

It's an on-going process and, sometimes, a fine juggling act. But, it's also well worth the effort involved.

If the author's book really takes off and he or she is invited to

New York for an appearance on network TV, or if the author is invited to another city for a personal appearance, the publicist should seize the moment and line up other appearances for that city. If air dates are known, a news release should be written and sent to the local press (including radio and TV news directors). Perhaps a book store appearance could also be scheduled.

Hot Spots

The publicist should keep track of geographic areas where the author's book does especially well. A periodic review of the central files will reveal this, as would a survey of sales slips. When hot spots are found, the publicist should jump on them and begin to line up appearances with the local media.

Chapter 13

Step-By-Step Procedures: A Review For The Publicist

Plan The Day

Each day must be planned. The publicist should know who to contact, who to write to, what media activities (if any) are planned, etc.

Towards this end, two items are an absolute must:

(1) A Large 'daily' desk calendar (the type where one day will take up both sides of the open pages is best) and,

(2) A large wall-mounted monthly, quarterly or yearly planning calendar. (Get the dry erasable type markers for the wall calendar.)

Interviews

The cycle of actions listed in the next few pages is the same cycle that must be repeated again and again by the publicist to line up and complete media interviews. The author should expect a few variations, as each interview booking is different.

The publicist should just take these steps one at a time. However, if troubles do crop up, the publicist should stop and consider them carefully for they indicate that something is wrong. Find whatever is wrong and fix it.

Personnel

The minimum personnel needed is one publicist and one author.

Beginning Actions For The Publicist

1. Determine the scope of the planned area of operation.

2. Acquire the appropriate media reference books or go to a library and seek information on the media sources within the planned area of operation.

3. Once this information has been obtained, complete the 3x5 cards for each media source in the planned area of operation.

4. Cross-reference the cards as needed.

5. Sort the 3x5 cards alphabetically and prepare a data sheet for each card, then sort them alphabetically.

6. Create and have printed a promotional flyer.

7. Take or gather any photographs necessary for the press kit. Make copies of as many thought necessary.

8. Obtain a good supply of brightly colored, glossy presentation folders (with inside pockets).

9. Obtain a supply of clear plastic 9x12 (freezer-type) bags or bright colored envelopes. (Note: the envelopes should be the same color as the presentation folders) and 5x7 or so white peel-away blank labels.

   a. Obtain a stamp or have return labels made up and neatly stamp the return address on the envelopes.

10. Formulate a generic media letter introducing the author and book. The letter should request interview air time: "Dear _____ Per our telephone conversation ..."

11. Make up a list of fifteen or twenty sample questions that reflect what the general public needs to know about the book.

12. Put a press kit together, and weight it along with the mailing envelope. Figure what postage will cost and budget money to match projected cost.

13. Allot the money for mailing the press kit (and possibly a book) to each radio and television station and major newspaper in the planned area of operation.

14. Once the first thirteen steps have been completed, contact the *first radio station* on the media list. (Note: Do not contact television stations at this time ... wait until experience is gained.)

    a. Does this station have a locally-produced talk show or shows that interview authors?

    b. If so, who are the producers?

    (Note this information on the data sheet.)

    c. Get in touch with a producer and attempt to sell this person on the idea of an interview.

    d. Follow what this person says (i.e. send information, call later or whatever).

NOTE: If there is no interest at this time from the first station or if the station does not have interview programs, note this information on the data sheet and go on to the next station.

If several stations have been called to no avail (not interested vs just booked up) stop and adjust the message somewhat. Something is turning the producers off.

The overall response will indicate if this is necessary.

    e. Transfer the information to the appropriate data sheet after the call and file in file folders.

REPEAT THE STEPS IN THIS SECTION UNTIL A BOOKING IS SCHEDULED OR SOMEONE REQUESTS THAT INFORMATION BE SENT.

NOTE EVERYTHING IN THE MEDIA FOLDERS.

KEEP THE MEDIA FOLDERS IN GOOD ORDER.

Press Kit and Cover Letter

1. Type up the generic cover letter, personalized to the producer.
2. Mail the press kit and cover letter.
3. On the data sheet, note the date that the press kit and cover letter were sent out and to whom.
4. Note the appropriate follow-up date on the desk calendar.

Stop and think about how all this fits together; how each action naturally flows to the next.

5. Begin contacting the remaining radio stations on the list.
6. Check the desk calendar daily and follow up as scheduled. Reschedule any incomplete actions. Update the cards and data sheets as necessary.
7. Confirm any interview show bookings by telephone one or two days in advance.
8. Arrive on time and author does the interview. Take a tape so that a copy can be made of the show.
9. With the author, critique the interview tape several days after the interview and decide on any changes that need to be made. Type up new sample questions to reflect these changes.

AUTHOR NOTE - THESE STEPS ARE CRUCIAL!

1. **MAKE <u>ANY</u> NECESSARY CHANGES.**
2. **<u>IF NECESSARY</u> GET ANOTHER PUBLICIST.**

Television Stations

1. Begin contacting television stations *after* several radio shows have been completed. But, if a TV station calls first, go for it! Follow the same steps necessary to line up the radio shows.

2. Take whatever actions are necessary to prepare the author for television, clothing, appearance, etc.

3. After a television show had been completed, stop and think about the differences between it and radio.

4. Resume contacting both radio and television stations.

Publicity Tours

1. Decide on the extent (how far and how long) of the tour.

2. Obtain local road maps.

3. Begin contacting the major media sources a minimum of two months in advance (three months for television).

4. Line up television and newstalk radio bookings first and then begin to fill in around them.

5. Begin plotting locations of the stations on the maps.

6. When there is a pretty good idea of just how long the trip will take, make any necessary hotel/motel, rent-a-car, flight reservations and budgeting plans. (Remember to budget for one or two days longer than the trip is planned for.)

7. Plan each day's schedule, coordinating it with the maps. Get directions from one location to the next and check on any road work in progress or anything else that might delay the schedule.

8. Confirm all reservations and bookings one week prior to leaving.

a. Be sure to notify each station or publication where interview bookings have been obtained of the local telephone number for messages.
 b. Reconfirm each station or publication interview twenty-four hours in advance.

9. Obtain and pack away any necessary medications, cough medicines, etc.

10. Ensure that someone at home base has an exact copy of the itinerary.

11. Arrive the day before the interviews are due to start.

12. Review the maps and the day's schedule early in the morning. Know the locations of each appointment and directions to it. Keep the big picture in mind.

13. Check in with the home office twice a day. Inform them of any changes.

14. Keep with the schedule, yet remain flexible. Remember that anything can (and might) happen. Be prepared to change the schedule if necessary. Do not fall into the trap of locking tightly into a schedule. There's nothing sacred about an itinerary.

It's Supposed To Be Fun!

Perhaps the best advice I could pass on is just to relax and have fun with the interviews. Nothing here is beyond the scope of anyone who has it together enough to write a book in the first place, and in the end it should all come down to having fun.

The only thing that differentiates the beginner from the professional is that the professional didn't give up and doesn't skip the basics.

Persistence, and determination, plus a small portion of talent are all that is required to get the job done, regardless of the size or complexity of the job.

Appendix

Rochester

Glossary

ACCESS: The availability of a media resource to the general public.

AIR TIME: Time spent on the air.

AM: Amplitude Modulation. As in AM Radio, which transmits by varying the amplitude (size) of its carrier wave in accordance with an encoded audio input signal. The AM broadcast band extends from 550 to 1600 kilohertz. Compare with 'FM.'

ANIMATED: The quality of someone being vibrant, full of zest; alive. Compare with 'dud.'

AREA OF COVERAGE: See 'Footprint.'

AREA OF OPERATION: The optimum area in which to operate for publicity purposes.

ASSOCIATE PRODUCER: The person responsible for producing certain segments of a particular TV or radio production, such as a cooking segment. Answers to the producer. For a big network show, there may be several associate producers, each doing one or more segments.

AUDIENCE: People viewing, reading or listening to a performance or work. Also, its demographic breakdown.

AUDIENCE COUNT: Estimated size of listening or viewing public, as established by various formulas. Compare with 'readership,' 'ratings,' and 'gross impressions.'

AUDIO: Sound.

AUTHORITY FACTOR: Term coined by author to represent that phenomenon wherein a person who observed an interview will, as a result, declare himself to be an expert on the subject of the interview. This person will often assume an authoritarian point of view and refer others to the subject or book in question, but it will hold little interest for himself.

BACKGROUND KIT: A folder containing biographical or historical information, press clippings, photographs, etc. for use by the media. Compare with 'press kit.'

BROADCAST AREA: See 'Footprint.'

BROADCAST STUDIO: The location from which a broadcast originates.

BROADCAST(ING): Broadcasting was originally a farming term, wherein a farmer would broadly cast his seed to all directions. Having to do with the people, industry and equipment that send radio and TV signals going to all directions. Compare with 'narrowcasting.'

BROADCAST TV: That operation which broadcasts television signals through the atmosphere. (As opposed to Cable TV.)

CABLECASTING: 'Broadcasting' something over cable wires. Also applies to major cable companies broadcasting to a satellite, which then relays the signal to a receiver at a cable company. The signal is then sent over the cable wires to individual customers.

CABLE TV: The industry that sends audio and video signals over closed-circuit telephone lines rather than through the atmosphere; narrowcasting.

CALL LETTERS: Identifying letters for all broadcast stations, such as 'KJAY FM,' 'KGO TV' for regular stations or 'K13UY' for translator stations.

CALL-IN SHOW: A radio or TV show wherein the audience can call in with live on the air comments or questions. Compare with talk show.

CAMERA SHY: Term describing a person with a fear of being on camera. Compare with 'mike fright.'

CARRIER WAVE: A wave of electromagnetic energy that can be modulated by amplitude, frequency, phase or other means to transmit electronic signals.

CHANNEL: A specific frequency band assigned to radio and TV stations. Radio stations are referred to by their assigned frequency, such as '1450 AM' or '93.9 FM.' TV stations use channel numbers, such as 'Channel 5' or 'Channel 36,' because each TV channel covers a specific band of frequencies. For example, the channel designated as '10' covers from 192-198 megacycles.

CHARM SCHOOL: Schools that prepare one for being interviewed. Sometimes offered by modeling agencies.

CITY OF LICENSE: The city to which a broadcast station is licensed. A station's broadcast studios do not necessarily have to be located in its city of license, as long as it can serve that city with a translator. Compare with 'city of origin.'

CITY OF ORIGIN: The city in which station has its primary broadcast studios. Compare with 'city of license.'

CLOSED-CIRCUIT: A electrical system that confines signals to itself as opposed to broadcasting them through the atmosphere. See 'narrowcasting.'

CLUTTER: See 'noise.'

CO-OWNED: Refers to more than one media outlet within a given market sharing a common owner.

COMBO: Short for combination, as in, "He owns an AM/FM combo." Multiple ownership of radio, TV and/or publications.

COMMERCIAL AIR TIME: Broadcast time that is paid for by commercial interests.

COMMERCIAL BREAK: A break in programming to air one or more commercial announcements.

COMMERCIAL: Paid-for advertising over radio and TV stations.

COMMUNITY ACCESS: Cable TV term wherein the company offers one or more channels to the community for its use. Contrast with 'local origination.'

COMMUNITY-ORIENTED: Term describing a broadcast station serving a small market, such as a rural area with a population of 20,000 or less. Such stations devote much of their programming to community-interest items, like garage sales, school announcements, farm reports and listener birthdays. Frequency usually 1400 & up (AM).

CONTACT PERSON: The person designated within the organization as the one to deal with the media. This person is seldom the organization's speaker, and is usually the publicist.

COPY: Written material, as in 'commercial copy.' Copy is written material that has been generated for a specific purpose.

COPYRIGHT: Legal term designating the person or entity who owns the rights to a given work or production for copy, sale or distribution. The copyright may be assigned by the owner to others. Owning a registered copyright protects the work from being infringed upon by others.

COVERAGE: Term designating the extent to which something is reported on or carried over the air.

CUE: To prompt for action. As in signalling a person that the microphone is live and he or she may begin.

CUE UP: To make ready for immediate air play, as in correctly positioning the needle on a record and placing the turntable in the stand-by mode in preparation for playing.

CUMULATIVE RESPONSE EFFECT: Term coined by the author to represent the condition that results from doing repeated interviews through the broadcast and print media over an extended period of time, and so keeping the book's name in front of the general public. Even the smallest, seemingly most insignificant, interview counts towards this. We can see this at work when orders begin to come in from people who never heard the interviews but were referred by others. (See also 'Hundreth Monkey Syndrome' and 'Authority Factor.')

CYCLES PER SECOND: Refers to the start, pulse, stop action of a transmitter pulsing with electromagnetic energy.

DEMOGRAPHICS: From demography, which is the study of the vital statistics of the human population and its characteristics. In broadcasting terms, it simply stands for the statistics and characteristics of the audience, whether actual or potential.

DIRECTOR: Person in charge of a specific area of a broadcast station, such as public affairs or the news department. The director is also responsible for keeping the department correctly focused. Answers to the program director.

DUB: (v) To reproduce an audio or video tape. (n) An audio or video tape so reproduced.

DUD: A person who is largely uncommunicative, unprofessional, and lacking in personality or sparkle.

DUD INTERVIEW: An interview that didn't work. Caused usually by a guest who was not up to par, although could also be caused by the air talent not being professional.

EDITOR: One who edits. A print media term roughly analogous to the broadcast industry's director. A publication will have editors for its various departments, such as health, education, city, national, etc. Editors are responsible for what the reporters produce.

EDITOR IN CHIEF: Print term denoting the chief editor - analogous to radio and TV program directors.

ELECTRONIC MEDIA: Term that applies to radio and television. Contrast with 'print media.'

ENGINEER: The engineer handles the technical end of a TV or radio production. In some smaller radio stations, the engineer might also double as a producer. By law, a station's chief engineer is also responsible for keeping all the FCC logs up to date and the equipment working within strict tolerances.

ENTERTAINMENT: Classification of programming, such as music or comedy as opposed to news, public affairs or religion.

EXECUTIVE PRODUCER: The person all the other producers answer to. Responsible for anything produced at the station.

FACT SHEET: Normally just one piece of paper that offers a quick-scan background regarding an individual or organization. A fact sheet would normally be included in press or background kits.

FAIRNESS DOCTRINE: A doctrine, eliminated in August of 1987 by the FCC, that required broadcast stations to not only air items of community importance, but to present both sides of any issue as well.

FAX: Short for 'facsimile' - a reproduction or exact copy of a document. Also, the electronic means for transferring these documents from one place to another.

FCC: Federal Communication Commission. The Federal agency that oversees the broadcast industry. Broadcasters and broadcast stations must be licensed by the FCC.

FEED: Features sent, usually by satellite or telephone lines to stations at prescribed times. As in 'news feed.'

FM: Frequency Modulation. As in FM Radio, which transmits its signal by varying the frequency of its carrier wave in accordance with an input signal. Compare with 'AM.'

FOOTAGE: A TV term, originally meaning the number of feet of exposed film a story contained. Now used loosely to indicate exposed video tape.

FOOTPRINT: A term that describes the area that a broadcast signal reaches: area of coverage. Generally measured on a radius out from a given station's broadcast antenna. The factors that generally define a given station's footprint are: terrain, frequency, broadcast power and atmospheric conditions. A given station's footprint can be from a few miles to hundreds or even thousands under the right conditions. Also known as 'broadcast area' or 'area of coverage.'

FORMAT: Each radio station will adapt a different format in order to reach a specific audience, such as country, newstalk, religious, or jazz. Also the material form and layout of a newspaper or publication.

FREQUENCY: The assigned channel of a radio station, expressed in cycles per second.

FREQUENCY BAND: The AM frequency band for North American radio stations is from 540 khz to 1600 KHz. Similarly, the FM band is from 88.1 MHz to 107.9 MHz.

GREEN ROOM: Off-stage room for radio and TV interview guests to relax before going on the air.

GROSS IMPRESSIONS: Advertising term. If one person sees one show or ad one time, that's one gross impression. If that same person sees the same show twice, or if someone else sees it once, that's two gross impressions, and so forth.

HARD NEWS: News that is currently happening or on-going; breaking stories. Contrast with 'soft news.'

HOG THE INTERVIEW: To not allow the other person a fair share of the interview. Both hosts and guests can hog the interview.

HOST: A unisex term, generally dealing with the on-air talent of an interview or game show.

HUNDREDTH MONKEY SYNDROME: Term referring to the phenomenon that occurs as the collective consciousness of a given population is increased. Beginning with a but few individuals, more and more members of the group begin to do, know or experience something until one day a critical level of consciousness is reached and suddenly all members of the group or population will join in. Compare with 'cumulative effect.'

HYPE: Deliberately misleading or exaggerated claims; disinformation.

I.D. : See 'station break.'

INTERN: Interns are usually college or broadcast school students who work, closely supervised, at radio and TV stations to further learn and refine their craft.

KHz: See 'kilohertz.'

KILOCYCLES: See 'kilohertz.'

KILOHERTZ (Khz): Thousand cycles per second. Refers to the frequency of AM radio stations. 610 Khz is a broadcast frequency of 610,000 cycles per second. Also known as 'kilocycles.' Compare with 'mega-hertz'

KISS METHOD: An old PR adage standing for Keep It Simple, Stupid. The less complicated something can be, the better it is.

LEAD TIME: Time given in advance of an event for promotional purposes. It helps to have several weeks to play with when promoting something, thus avoiding 'too little, too late' conflicts.

LIVE: Not taped or recorded. The viewer or listener is experiencing the performance as it is occurring.

LIVE ON TAPE: Program recorded live for use at a later date. Actually a misleading term. Programs are either live or taped.

LOCAL ORIGINATION: Cable TV station that originates programming of its own over one or more channels. Sometimes includes audio that is channeled through FM radios, but still carried over the cable system. Access is not necessarily offered to the community. Contrast with 'community access.'

LOGO I.D. : A slogan that identifies a particular station and is usually built around the call letters or frequency: 'Magic 61' (KFRC AM 610) or 'The Rocker' (KRQR FM).

LOW POWER TELEVISION (LPTV): Television translator stations that are permitted by the FCC to originate programming of a limited nature. They are not permitted to interfere in any way with normal broadcast TV stations.

MEDIA: The term 'media' is plural for 'medium' which, in this case, has to do with mass communication; radio, TV, periodicals and newspapers.

MEDIA CONTACT: In the context of media promotions, this is any person who must be dealt with at a media resource in order to obtain media coverage.

MEDIA KIT: A promotional package put together for the benefit of media personnel; usually contains a news release, background material, a biography (if applicable), assorted press clippings and possibly a series of suggested questions. Also called a 'press kit.'

MEDIA OUTLET: Radio station, TV station, periodical, newspaper or Cable TV station offering public access. Same as 'media source' or 'media resource.'

MEDIA PLAN: To be successful at media publicity, one must go about it in a planned, logical fashion, as opposed to an unplanned haphazard approach.

MEDIA SOURCE: Same thing as 'media outlet.'

MEGACYCLE: Term indicating a million cycles per second.

MEGAHERTZ: An FM station having a frequency of 107.9 MHz broadcasts at the rate of 107,900 million cycles per second. Written as MHz. See also 'megacycle.'

MEDIA SOURCE: See 'media outlet.'

MESSAGE: (see PR Message)

MHz: See 'megahertz'

MIKE FRIGHT: Microphone fright is radio's version of 'camera shy.' Someone who has 'mike fright' will never make it in the creative end of radio and certainly would never make a good interview subject.

NARROWCASTING: A term largely applied to the cable TV industry. Also applies to any closed-circuit audio or video production such as pay TV. Compare with 'broadcasting' and 'cablecasting.'

NETWORK: A group of allied TV or radio stations such as NBC (National Broadcasting Company) or NPR (National Public Radio). Networks are usually nationwide but can also be regional, such as the South Dakota News Network. There are radio, TV and Cable TV networks.

NEWSTALK: Stations that have a format consisting of news and talk shows exclusively. (Sometimes written as news/talk.)

NOISE: An electronic disturbance that reduces or completely obscures the clarity or understandability of a signal. In advertising or Promotions, 'noise' is information from other advertising or promotional sources that competes with a given piece of information for the attention of the projected public - also known as 'clutter.'

NUMBERS GAME: Ratings; audience count. Term referring to the actions taken to establish and garner ever higher ratings.

OPPOSING VIEWPOINT: The opposite side to any issue. Reporters will usually seek out any opposing viewpoints to a story that is controversial in nature.

PATCH CORD: Cords used to connect two circuits. An old-style telephone switchboard used patch cords. In newer equipment, patch cords are often replaced by electronic switches.

PILOT/PILOT SHOW: A show that is shot, filmed or recorded for the express purpose of being considered for a series.

PLAYBACK: To view or listen to what was just recorded on tape.

PR: (n) Public relations. Can also mean someone who works in public relations or even as a publicist. (v) The term is also used to indicate hype, as in "They really tried to PR me."

PRE-INTERVIEW: A brief interview, sometimes conducted just prior to the actual interview, in which the guest is briefed on the questions that will be asked. This also gives the show host time to get acquainted with the guest and allows the guest time to calm down before the interview begins. Some pre-interviews will be conducted by the producer or an interne, with the show's host absent.

PRESS AGENT: See 'publicist.'

PRESS CLIPPINGS: Articles cut from newspapers, usually collected and saved by the concerned parties.

PRESS KIT: See 'media kit.'

PRESS RELEASE: Formal release of information to the media. Also called 'news release.'

PRIMA DONNA: As used in this book, interview guests who have an inflated ego. They are usually conceited, difficult to interview and temperamental. Can also be show host who hogs the interview.

PRINT MEDIA: Those who print periodicals. Refers to the newspaper and magazine industries.

PRODUCER: As referred to in this book, one who produces something, such as news or interviews within the electronic media. The producer is responsible for the entire production and everyone on it as well as for booking interviews. Sometimes public affairs programming is produced by independent producers, whose only connection with the stations is that they provide programming and answer to the public affairs director. (See also 'associate producer.')

PROFESSIONAL: One who attains, and then maintains, the highest standards of technical expertise, skill and conduct in a particular field.

PROGRAM DIRECTOR (PD): The program director is the senior director within broadcast stations and is responsible for all the programming. Answers to the general manager or owner only.

PROGRAMMING DEPARTMENT: The department within radio and TV stations that is responsible for everything that goes over the air; all the station's programs. The programming department is headed by the program director.

PROMOTIONS: As used in this book, the actions taken to promote or publicize something through the media.

PUBLIC: An unorganized group of people bonded by a common interest, such as readers who buy a certain book. In radio and TV terms, this is the listening or viewing audience. In print media terminology, the readership.

PUBLIC BROADCASTING: That segment of the broadcast industry that operates on a non-commercial basis for the good of the community. Supported by private donations, governmental, public and private industry grants.

PUBLIC RELATIONS: The science or art of developing and maintaining good relations with the public. Quite often, an organization's publicist can be found in the public relations department.

PUBLICATIONS: The print media.

PUBLICIST: One who publicizes. The publicist is the person who contacts the media in order to promote something. Sometimes called a 'PR,' but also known as a 'publicity' or 'press' agent.

PUBLICITY: Information that is disseminated through various means, such as radio, TV and periodicals, with the intent of attracting public attention.

PUBLICITY AGENT: See 'publicist.'

RADIO STATION: Business licensed by the FCC for the broadcasting of encoded electromagnetic audio signals in a specific AM or FM frequency band. (Compare with 'narrowcasting.')

RATINGS: How a station compares with other stations. Determined by different audience surveys. Advertising rates are generally based upon the ratings. Also known as 'numbers.'

READERS: See 'readership.'

READERSHIP: Known or estimated number of people reading a given publication - determined by subscription count and surveys.

RECORD: (v) To record something is to apply sound and/or visual signals to audio or video tape or compact disc by electrical means, for preservation and eventual playback.

SCHEDULING CALENDER: A monthly or yearly wall calender used by the publicist for planning and scheduling media or public relations actions.The scheduling calender is vital to successful media planning.

SECOND-PARTY RESPONSE: The response from media exposure that comes in to an organization on a referral basis. The party that actually heard a given interview on a book will not necessarily seek out the subject book, but will refer it to others. See also, 'authority factor.'

SET: Regularly-scheduled television shows are usually shot on a sound stage location that is permanently 'set' up for that particular show. A typical set would consist of a backdrop and two or three chairs set up on a four inch elevated platform or 'riser.' Completing the set might be a coffee table and a vase with flowers. Some sets such as those for news shows or morning TV shows like, "Good Morning America" can be very elaborate. Compare with 'studio' and 'sound stage.'

SHOOT/SHOT: To record an interview or anything not previously recorded on video tape for later use. A remote location taping is sometimes referred to as a 'shoot.'

SHOW BUSINESS: That business concerned primarily with entertainment. With radio and TV, show business can also be concerned with education as well.

SIGNAL: As in broadcast signal. Modulated electromagnetic waves encoded with information. The signal is what is received by a radio or TV and then converted into sound and/or video.

SIMULCAST: Broadcast industry term for 'simultaneous broadcast,' referring to the action of a radio and television station simultaneously broadcasting a common event, such as a concert. Also refers to a station duplicating its sister station's signal (a common practice for AM/FM combos).

SISTER STATION: A station that is owned in concert with one or more other stations.

SOUND STAGE: A large, soundproof room used for the taping or filming of something, such as specials or commercials. Compare with 'studio' and 'set.'

SPOT: A short, usually commercial, announcement.

START DATE: The actual or requested beginning date for an announcement or series.

STATION BREAK: A scheduled break in programming, in which a station identifies itself, its frequency and city of license.

STUDIO: A small room in which radio or TV personalities perform and are recorded or aired live. In radio, sometimes called 'broadcast booth.' Compare with 'sound stage' and 'set.'

SUBJECT/TOPIC: The basis for an interview. The subject or topic is usually generalized, whereas the guest's message will be more specific. For instance, the topic might be on 'the plight of the homeless,' where the guest's message might be, "Here's a book on how to solve the plight of the homeless." Contrast with 'message.'

TALENT: In broadcast terms, the person who is actually on the air. Also called 'air personality,' a term that is rapidly replacing 'disc jockey' within the industry. Can also apply to guests (see 'talent coordinator').

TALENT COORDINATOR: The person often assigned to do any pre-interviews with guests ('talent'). Answers to the associate producer or producer. This person will often be responsible for herding the guests around the TV studio as their individual segments come up.

TALK SHOW: A broadcast interview, sometimes with the capability of taking on-the-air calls.

TAPE: Magnetic tape used for recording audio or audio and visual signals together. Usually designated as simply 'tape' for audio, and 'video tape' for a combination of audio and video.

TELEVISION STATION: Business licensed by the FCC for the broadcasting of encoded audio and video electromagnetic signals on an assigned channel. (Compare with 'narrowcasting.')

THEME: The topic of an interview show. Can also be broadly taken to represent a show's overall direction.

TRANSLATOR: A secondary station that rebroadcasts the signal of its parent station, thereby extending the parent station's range into remote areas it would not otherwise be able to serve. Translator call signs are different from normal broadcast stations (e.g. K13UY).

TRANSMITTER: The piece of equipment that transmits radio or TV signals by generating and amplifying an electrical carrier wave, combining it with a signal that is derived from voice or electrical impulses and then broadcasts (radiates) that signal from an antenna.

TV SET: An electronic instrument capable of receiving and displaying broadcast or narrowcast audio and video signals.

VIDEO: Dealing with vision.

WINDOW OF OPPORTUNITY; Refers to the time span in which an interview can be undertaken.

WORK SOMEONE: An attempt to garner support for an idea through persuasion. Used in a negative context, as in cult members attempting to work the press at a press conference. A practice used extensively by cults and political activists.

YUPPER/NUPPER: An interview guest who consistently answers in a monosyllabic fashion. The term comes from the guest answering 'yup' or 'nope' to questions and then not expanding any further. The most dreaded type of guest to a show host.

Bibliography

Babbie, Earl.
You Can Make A Difference.
St. Martin's Press 1985, New York, New York.

Bach, Richard.
Illusions, The Adventures of a Reluctant Messiah.
Dell Publishing Co., Inc. 1977. New York, New York.

Reed Publishing, Inc.
Broadcasting & Cable Marketplace.
New Providence, NJ. Published Annually.

Gale Research Company.
Gale Directory of Publications and Broadcast Media.
Detroit, Michigan (Formerly IMS/Ayer Directory of Publications). Published Annually.

Keyes, Ken, Jr.
Hundredth Monkey.
Vision Books, 1982. Coos Bay, OR

Millman, Dan.
Way of the Peaceful Warrior.
H.J. Kramer, Inc., 1980, 1984, Tiburon, CA.

Rochester

Acknowledgements

Where to start? The list of people who have had sufficient influence to affect what went into this book is extensive - far too extensive to list. But, you know who you are, and you know I appreciate the input. However, I would like to mention a few of the really special people who never gave up on me; their support and love has kept me going. They are, in no particular order:

Carol Rochester, my mother and probably the best friend I'll ever have, who has stood by me through thick and thin. I'll always love her;

Bob Bare, friend for life, editor, publisher of this book and co-author with me of other books to follow; Joanie, Mariah, and Dan Bare (Bob's family), who taught me that laughter is still possible, even under the most horrendous of conditions;

Karen Grech, a dear friend since we first spent a magical night beneath the redwoods in Big Sur in 1969;

Thanks to the management and staff of K9-FM in Redding, California.

Sheena and Dana Ferree, delightful young women who embraced me into their lives and accepted me as a friend without hesitation;

Dee Gretzler, who taught me about the joy of life;

Ron and Alice Davis who taught me what true friendship means;

Fatima Ali, wise and wonderful woman who taught me the meaning of patience;

Thanks to the management and staff of KFRC-AM Radio in San Francisco.

Lynn Dubonis, who accepted me as a friend and helped me through many a tough day;

Carl Schwahn, whose humor has kept me afloat through many dark times;

'Do' and Betty Doty and their sidekick Rebecca Merideth who have steered me past many dangerous shoals in the publishing world;

Robin Fahr, who taught me the meaning of integrity;

Frank 'Sarge' Gerbode, M.D. and Gerald French, again, teachers of integrity and good humor;

Dan Poynter, author of <u>The Self Publishing Manual</u> who opened my eyes to the best way to publish a book;

Sally Hall-Dubois, who taught me that people are meant to smile and laugh, after all, and

Richard Bach, author and visionary, for the inspiration that led to this book becoming a reality.

Thank you one and all. I love you.

Larry J. Rochester
August, 1992

Index

ACCESS   135
AIR TIME   135
AM   135
AM Radio   135
ANIMATED   135
assigned frequency   137
ASSOCIATE PRODUCER   135
AUDIENCE   135
AUDIO   135

BACKGROUND KIT   136
BROADCAST AREA
   See 'Footprint.'   136
BROADCAST STUDIO   136

Cable TV   138
CABLECASTING   136
CALL-IN SHOW   136
CAMERA SHY   136
CARRIER WAVE   137
CHANNEL   137
CITY OF LICENSE   137
city of license   137
city of origin   137
CLOSED-CIRCUIT   137
CLUTTER   137
clutter   144
CO-OWNED   137
COMMERCIAL AIR TIME   137
COMMERCIAL BREAK   137
commercial copy   138
common owner   137
COMMUNITY ACCESS   138
COMMUNITY-ORIENTED   138
COPYRIGHT   138
CUE   138
cumulative effect   142
CUMULATIVE RESPONSE EFFECT   138

DEMOGRAPHICS   139
DIRECTOR   139
DUB   139

DUD   139
dud   135
DUD INTERVIEW   139

EDITOR   139
EDITOR IN CHIEF   139
ELECTRONIC MEDIA   139
ENGINEER   139
ENTERTAINMENT   140
EXECUTIVE PRODUCER   140

FACT SHEET   140
FAX   140
FCC
   Federal Communication Commission.   140
FEED   140
FM   140

Gale Research Company   151
GREEN ROOM   141

HARD NEWS   141
HUNDREDTH MONKEY SYNDROME   141

I.D.   142
INTERN
   college or broadcast school students   142

KHz   142
KILOCYCLES   142
KILOHERTZ (Khz)   142
KISS METHOD   142

LIVE   142
LIVE ON TAPE   142
LOCAL ORIGINATION   142
local origination   138

MEDIA   143
MEDIA KIT   143
MEDIA PLAN   143
media producer   6
media resource   135
MEDIA SOURCE   143
MEGAHERTZ   143

MESSAGE   143
MHz   144
MIKE FRIGHT   144
mike fright   137

NARROWCASTING   144
narrowcasting   136, 137
NETWORK   144
NEWSTALK   144
noise   137
NUMBERS GAME   144

OPPOSING VIEWPOINT   144

PILOT/PILOT SHOW   144
PRE-INTERVIEW   145
PRESS AGENT   145
PRESS CLIPPINGS   145
PRESS KIT   145
press kit   136
PRIMA DONNA   145
PRINT MEDIA   145
PRODUCER   145
PROFESSIONAL   146
PROGRAM DIRECTOR (PD)   146
PROGRAMMING DEPARTMENT   146
PUBLIC BROADCASTING   146
PUBLIC RELATIONS   146
PUBLICATIONS   146
PUBLICIST   146
publicist   138
PUBLICITY AGENT   147

RADIO STATION   147
RATINGS   147
ratings   135
READERS   147
READERSHIP   147
readership ratings   135
RECORD   147

SCHEDULING CALENDER   147
SECOND-PARTY RESPONSE   147
SHOOT/SHOT   148
SHOW BUSINESS   148

Rochester

SISTER STATION   148
SOUND STAGE   148
SPOT   148
START DATE   148
STATION BREAK   148

TALENT COORDINATOR   149
TALK SHOW   149
talk show   136
TAPE   149
TELEVISION STATION   149
translator   137
TRANSMITTER   149
TV SET   149

VIDEO   150

YUPPER/NUPPER   150